THE COMPLETE STEP-BY-STEP GUIDE TO
CAKE DECORA

CREATIVE
PUBLISHING
international

www.creativepub.com

THE COMPLETE STEP-BY-STEP GUIDE TO
CAKE DECORATING

40 stunning cakes for all occasions

Carol Deacon

First published in 2003 in the USA and Canada by
Creative Publishing international, Inc.

18705 Lake Drive East
Chanhassen, Minnesota 55317
1-800-328-3895
www.creativepub.com

President/CEO: Michael Eleftheriou
Vice President/Publisher: Linda Ball
Vice President/Retail Sales: Kevin Haas

First published in 2003 by
New Holland Publishers (UK) Ltd
London • Cape Town • Sydney • Auckland

Senior Editor: Clare Hubbard
Designer: Isobel Gillan
Photographer: Shona Wood
Additional photography: Edward Allwright and Chris Turner
Additional steps and cake shots: Janice Murfitt
Editorial Direction: Rosemary Wilkinson
Production: Hazel Kirkman

ISBN 1-58923-086-8 (softcover)

Reproduction by Modern Age Repro House Ltd, Hong Kong
Printed and bound in Malaysia by Times Offset (M) sdn Bhd

10 9 8 7 6 5 4 3 2 1

NOTES
Because of the slight risk of salmonella, raw eggs should not be served to the
very young, the ill or elderly, or to pregnant women.

In the recipes use either metric or imperial measurements, but never a combination of
the two, as exact conversions are not always possible.

ACKNOWLEDGEMENTS
Carol Deacon would like to thank Pamela Eve, Elyane, Paul, Stephen, Rosie and Holly Jones
and Juliette and Charlie for their help "Twiggy sitting" during the making of this book. Carol
would also like to thank Valerie Hedgethorne for her marzipan recipe on page 84.

The cake shown on page 2 is the Wedding star (see pages 104–105).

CONTENTS

INTRODUCTION

Probably the most commonly uttered phrase when a decorated cake is brought out at a celebration is "Oh isn't that lovely...", quickly followed by "I could never do that!" Well, guess what? Neither could I, once.

The secret behind successful cake decorating is not having a steady hand, an eye for color, a creative mother or any of the other excuses that I've heard over the years. In fact, there are really only two secrets to cake decorating. The first is to give it a try, and the second is to allow yourself enough time.

However, just launching yourself up the home baking aisle in the supermarket or into your nearest cake decorating equipment supplier with no real idea of what to buy will result in bewilderment, frustration and, quite possibly, an empty space on the table where a cake should be. So here's how the *Complete Step-by-Step Guide to Cake Decorating* can help you.

From baking the perfect sponge cake to icing a wedding cake, I have explained and demystified many of the techniques used, to create simple but stunning cakes. This is not the most technical cake book on the market but that's because I have tried to take the simplest route to a great end result without scaring anyone!

Primarily this book is aimed at the beginner or those with a little experience who want to take their skills further. However, because some of the ideas are so simple and quick, it will also appeal to those with years of experience, too. After all, you may be the most experienced cake decorator in the world but I bet you still get asked to produce things at the last minute!

It is easy to forget that cooking, especially preparing special items like this, is not knowledge that any of us is born with. It involves reading, learning and practice. However, I believe that learning should be enjoyable, information understandable and great results easily attainable.

So, now you are about to learn a lot of new things that you never knew you wanted to know. But best of all, you are about to bring joy to a lot of people. Just watch their faces light up when you bring out your creation and I bet if you listen carefully you'll hear the odd whisper of "Oh isn't that lovely...I could never do that!"

Carol Deacon

BAKING BASICS

This section gives you all of the basic information that you need to know before you actually start making the cake. There is advice on what you need to think about before you start, cake sizes and portions, information on baking pans and how to line them and a fail-safe way of calculating how much mixture you need. Basically, you'll find everything you need to know to get you started.

There are certain questions that you need to think about beforehand to ensure that the finished cake is everything that you wanted it to be:

* How many people will the cake need to serve?
* What sort of cake does/do the recipient/s like?
* What style of cake is needed?
* How much time have you got?
* Are there things you can do in advance?

Cake sizes and portions

To get the maximum number of portions out of a cake, it is best to cut it into rectangles rather than wedges.

To give you an idea of the size of cake you should be baking, opposite is a guide to the approximate number of portions you can get from cakes of various sizes.

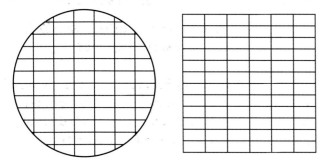

ABOVE *These diagrams show the best way to cut a round and a square cake.*

Cutting cakes

To be sure you have enough to feed everyone, a cutting cake can be made. This cake does not have any decoration on it. It should be made to match the main cake—fruit, sponge, chocolate or whatever and covered with the same kind of icing, but it is then left plain, as it will never be shown. It is especially useful at weddings to have a spare cake like this to provide lots of extra slices.

SIZE AND PORTION GUIDE		
	Sponge Cake	Fruit Cake
6" (15cm) round	10	20
6" (15cm) square	15	25
7" (18cm) round	15	30
7" (18 cm) square	20	40
8" (20cm) round	20	40
8" (20cm) square	25	50
9" (23cm) round	25	50
9" (23cm) square	35	70
10" (25cm) round	30	65
10" (25cm) square	45	90
11" (28cm) round	40	85
11" (28cm) square	55	110
12" (30cm) round	50	100
12" (30cm) square	65	130

Baking pans

There are all sorts of pans available for baking cakes. Some are rigid all-in-one pans, others have a spring-release mechanism that releases the sides of the pan, freeing the cake and others have a separate top and side section that allows you to push the cake out of the pan when baked. There is also an increasing range of shaped pans available, from numbers and letters, hearts and stars, to cartoon characters. There is no hard and fast rule as to what type of pan (spring-release, rigid etc.) is best for a particular cake. You just need to ensure that whatever size or shape of pan you use will provide you with enough cake for your chosen design.

Lining a cake pan

Lining a cake pan sometimes seems like the most tedious part of the whole cake-making process, but it really is the only way to ensure that all of your cake comes out of the pan in one piece. There are a couple of new products on the market, "cake sprays" that claim that if you use them there is no need to line your pan. I can't comment on whether they are effective or not as I've never used them, I prefer to line my pans.

Some kitchen and specialty stores sell paper cake pan liners which you simply put in the pan with no need to add grease of any sort. One has been used in the Monster chocolate cup cake on page 132 and even becomes part of the finished creation.

You can use either wax paper or baking parchment to line the pan. The only difference is that the baking parchment does not need to be greased.

1 Measure the circumference and height of the pan. Cut out a strip of wax paper or baking parchment to that length and about 1" (2.5 cm) wider than the height of the pan.

2 Place the pan onto another piece of paper or parchment and draw around the base. Cut out the drawn shape.

3 Wipe a little butter or margarine around the inside of the pan.

4 Place the long strip around the inside of the pan (Fig. a). Slip the other piece into the bottom of the pan.

a

Lining a cake pan for fruit cake

The method for lining a pan ready for baking a fruit cake is exactly the same as for a sponge cake, except that you need to double line the pan. This protects the sides and base of the cake during its long cooking time. So cut out two strips for the sides and two base pieces.

It is also advisable to wrap a double layer of brown or wax paper around the outside of the pan. Tie string around the outside to hold it in place (Fig. b).

b

How to calculate how much mixture is needed for an unusual shaped pan

Not all cake pans are square or round. Here's a handy tip to work out how much cake mixture you need.

1 Fill a cup with water. Tip the water into the pan. Repeat until the water has reached the level that the unbaked cake mixture would reach if the pan were filled. Usually about 1" (2.5 cm) from the top. Count the cupfuls.

2 Now take a cake pan for which you know how much cake mixture would be needed. For instance, an 8" (20-cm) round pan which would take a four-egg sponge mixture. Using the same cup, count how many cupfuls of water would be needed to fill that pan.

3 If the number of cupfuls to fill the unusual shaped pan is double the cupfuls required to fill the 8" (20-cm) round pan, then you know that you need to make double the quantity of cake mixture. If it is half, then you know you need to make half, and so on.

CAKE RECIPES

In the rush to get to the exciting, decorating part, it is easy to overlook the baking. However, no matter how exotic the cake looks, a cake is made to be eaten and it absolutely has to taste as good as it looks. Here are some basic cake recipes which are my reliable favorites and they always taste great.

Madeira sponge

This sponge cake recipe is extremely easy. You just put all the ingredients in a bowl and mix. A food mixer makes light work of the mixing and takes only a minute. It will take longer if you're mixing by hand. To make things easier for yourself, make sure the butter is very soft.

INGREDIENTS				
SQUARE PAN		6" (15cm)	7" (18cm)	8" (20cm)
ROUND PAN	6" (15cm)	7" (18cm)	8" (20cm)	9" (23cm)
Self-raising flour	1½c (175g)	1¾c (225g)	2¼c (285g)	2¾c (350g)
Sugar	½c (115g)	¾c (170g)	1c (230g)	1⅓c (285g)
Butter (softened)	½c (115g)	⅔c (170g)	1c (230g)	1¼c (285g)
Eggs (medium)	2	3	4	5
Milk	1tbsp (15ml)	1tbsp (15ml)	2tbsp (30ml)	3tbsp (45ml)
Baking time (approx)	1¼–1½hrs	1¼–1½hrs	1½–1¾ hrs	1½–2 hrs

1 Grease and line the relevant cake pan (see page 8) and preheat your oven to 300°F/150°C. (Timings and temperatures for fan-assisted ovens may vary. Refer to your manufacturer's handbook for guidance.)

2 Sift the flour into a mixing bowl to get some air into it and add all the rest of the ingredients.

3 Set the mixer to a slow setting and slowly bind all of the ingredients together.

4 Increase the speed and beat for a minute until the mixture has become pale and silky.

5 Spoon the mixture into a prepared pan and smooth the top.

6 Bake for the required time. When ready, the cake should have pulled away slightly from the edges of the pan. If pressed lightly, the top should spring back from the touch. Insert a sharp knife or cake skewer into the cake. If it comes out clean, the cake is ready.

7 Turn the cake out of the pan, upside down onto a cooling rack. Peel off the lining and leave to cool.

STORING: Ice cake when cool or wrap in plastic wrap until ready. Use and eat within five days.
FREEZING: Once baked and cooled, this sponge can be frozen for up to three months.

Flavor variations
CHOCOLATE Add a tablespoon of cocoa powder in place of a tablespoon of flour for a quick chocolate sponge.
ORANGE/LEMON For a hint of citrus, add the grated zest of an orange or lemon before baking.
ALMOND Add a teaspoon of extract to the basic mixture.
COCONUT Add ⅔ cup (60 g) flaked coconut to the mixture.

Pudding bowl, sandwich and fairy cakes

Use the three-egg sponge mixture to make a 1-quart (1-litre) pudding bowl cake for the Monster cup cake (see page 132), 24 fairy cakes for the Fearsome dragon (see page 70) or two sandwich cakes for the Quick chocolate cake on page 120.

Make sure the pudding bowl is heatproof. Grease the inside and place a disc of wax paper in the base. When the cake is cooked, slide a palette knife around the edge of the bowl to release it. Tip onto a cooling rack and peel off the wax paper disc. If you don't have a bowl, bake a round cake and carve it into a rounded shape.

RIGHT *Fairy cakes are fun, easy to make and can be decorated in many different ways.*

Chocolate cake

This cake takes a little more effort than the simple chocolate sponge recipe on page 10, but the velvet texture of the finished cake makes the trouble worthwhile. A crust will form on the top of the cake as it cooks, it might even scorch slightly. Don't worry, this is normal and will not affect the taste of the cake underneath. Slice the crust off the cake after it has cooled and just before decorating.

INGREDIENTS				
SQUARE PAN		6" (15cm)	7" (18cm)	8" (20cm)
ROUND PAN	6" (15cm)	7" (18cm)	8" 20cm)	9" (23cm)
Butter (softened)	⅓c (90g)	½c (115g)	⅔c (170g)	1c (230g)
Sugar	3tbsp (40g)	⅓c (75g)	½c (115g)	⅔c (150g)
Eggs (medium)	3	4	6	8
Plain chocolate	5oz (150g)	6oz (170g)	8oz (230g)	10oz (285g)
Self-raising flour	¾c (90g)	1c (115g)	1⅓c (170g)	1¾c (230g)
Powdered sugar	¼c (30g)	¼c (30g)	½c (60g)	⅔c (90g)
Baking time (approx)	45–55 mins	45mins–1 hr	1–1¼ hrs	1–1¼ hrs

1 Grease and line the relevant cake pan (see pages 8–9) and preheat the oven to 350°F/180°C. (Timings and temperatures for fan-assisted ovens may vary. Refer to your manufacturer's handbook for guidance.)

2 Separate the egg whites from the yolks and set aside in two small bowls.

3 Melt the chocolate in a heatproof bowl (see page 114).

4 In a mixing bowl, cream the softened butter and sugar together.

5 Beat in the egg yolks and then the melted chocolate.

6 Set the mixer to a low speed and slowly stir in the flour. Stop as soon as it has all been incorporated. Set aside.

7 Put the egg whites into a second mixing bowl. Connect the whisk attachment to your mixer and whisk the egg whites until stiff. Whisk in the powdered sugar.

8 Reattach the beater to the mixer and slowly stir the chocolate mixture into the egg whites.

9 Pour into a prepared pan and bake immediately. The crust on top of the cake can make it difficult to tell if the cake is cooked by touch alone so carefully cut a little section of crust away from the center of the cake. Insert a knife or cake skewer. If it comes out clean, the cake is ready.

10 Turn the cake out onto a cooling rack. Remove the wax paper and leave to cool.

STORING: Ice within a day of baking. If this is not possible, freeze until required.
FREEZING: When cooled, this cake will freeze well for up to three months. Leave the crust on if freezing.

LEFT *Quick chocolate cake (see page 120).*

Special effects with sponge cake

Forget decorating for a moment, there are a few special effects that can be achieved with the cake itself.

Checkered sponge

This effect is fun, as from the outside it looks like an ordinary cake, but when you cut into it you have a checkered effect. You need two round sponge cakes of contrasting colors; usually a plain sponge and a chocolate sponge are used.

1 Using cutters, cut two circles out of the plain sponge. Do the same with the chocolate cake (Fig. a).

2 Before assembling the cake, coat the inside of each piece with buttercream or jam. Swap the middles around—so the middle of the chocolate cake goes into the middle of the plain sponge and vice versa (Fig. b).

3 Sandwich the cakes together with your chosen filling (Fig. c).

a b c

Striped sponge

This is another way of adding interest to the cake itself. Children particularly like the surprise of seeing the unexpected when the cake is cut. You need two round sponge cakes of contrasting colors; usually a plain sponge and a chocolate sponge are used.

1 Cut each cake in half. Reassemble the cake by sandwiching together the plain and chocolate sponge pieces in alternate layers (Fig. d).

2 You can use your filling of choice to assemble the layers. Try to keep the layers as level as possible (Fig. e).

d e

Fruit cake

I've said this before, but I'll say it again as it's so true—there is absolutely nothing to beat the seasonal aroma of cinnamon and spices wafting through the house in the dreary winter months before Christmas. Visitors to your home will not only want to stir the mixture and make a wish, but they'll start telling you tales of how they used to visit their grannies when they were young, how she used to bake wonderful cakes and before you know it, you will have spread Christmas spirit without even trying.

Making your own fruit cake is a lot easier than you might think. The secret is to make sure you've got everything together before you start.

INGREDIENTS				
SQUARE PAN	6" (15cm)	7" (18cm)	8" (20cm)	9" (23cm)
ROUND PAN	7" (18cm)	8" (20cm)	9" (23cm)	10" (25cm)
Currants	¾c (150g)	1c (175g)	1¼c (200g)	1⅓c (225g)
Raisins	¾c (150g)	1c (175g)	1¼c (200g)	1⅓c (225g)
Sultanas	¾c (150g)	1c (175g)	1¼c (200g)	1⅓c (225g)
Mixed peel	2tbsp (30g)	¼c (45g)	⅓c (60g)	½c (75g)
Candied cherries	¼c (60g)	5tbsp (75g)	⅓c (90g)	½c (100g)
Brandy	4tbsp (60ml)	6tbsp (90ml)	8tbsp (120ml)	8tbsp (120ml)
Butter(softened)	⅔c (150g)	¾c (175g)	¾c (200g)	1c (225g)
Sugar (soft, dark brown)	⅔c (150g)	¾c (175g)	1c (200g)	1¼c (225g)
Eggs (medium)	3	4	5	6
Plain flour	1⅓c (175g)	1⅔c (200g)	1¾c (225g)	2¼c (270g)
Mixed spice	2 tsp	2 tsp	1 tbsp	1 tbsp
Cinnamon	½ tsp	½ tsp	¾ tsp	1 tsp
Lemon (zest only)	½	½	1	1
Ground almonds	3tbsp (20g)	¼c (30g)	⅓c (45g)	½c (60g)
Flaked almonds	3tbsp (20g)	¼c (30g)	⅓c (45g)	½c (60g)
Baking time (approx)	1½–2 hrs	1¾–2¼ hrs	2–2¼ hrs	2¼–2¾ hrs

1 Place all the dried fruits into a bowl and pour the brandy over them. Stir and cover the bowl with a plate. Leave the fruits to soak for a few hours, preferably overnight.

2 Prepare the cake pan (see page 9) and preheat the oven to 300°F/150°C. (Timings and temperatures for fan-assisted ovens may vary. Refer to your manufacturer's handbook for guidance.)

3 Cream the butter and sugar together, then beat in the eggs.

4 Slowly mix in the sifted flour, spices and ground almonds. Add a little more flour if it seems too runny.

5 Stir in the soaked fruits, lemon zest and flaked almonds. Spoon the mixture into the prepared pan. Smooth the surface and bake.

6 Check the cake 15–20 minutes before the end of the baking time. If the top is turning very brown, place a disc of wax paper over the top.

7 To test the cake, insert a sharp knife or cake skewer. If it comes out clean, the cake is done.

8 Allow the cake to cool completely in the pan. If using the cake right away, turn it out of the pan when cooled and remove the paper.

STORING: You can store this cake for up to three months. When cooled, tip it out of the baking pan and leave the wax paper around the sides. Poke a few holes in the top of the cake with a cocktail stick and drizzle over some brandy. Let the brandy soak in and then wrap the cake in two sheets of wax paper. Double wrap it again using two sheets of aluminum foil and place in a box or cupboard until required. Do not store it in a plastic airtight container as this can encourage mold growth. You can "feed" your cake every one to two weeks with a little more brandy if you wish.

FREEZING: If you plan to keep the cake longer than three months, wrap in wax paper and freeze until required. Defrost thoroughly for about 8 hours at room temperature.

Microwave cakes

In case of emergency, here are a couple of cakes you can cook in four minutes! The texture is slightly different from that of oven-baked cakes and the vanilla cake will look pale as it will not brown on the top. Never use a metal cake pan in a microwave oven.

Vanilla cake
This recipe is for a 7" (18-cm) round microwave cake dish or a l-litre (2-pint) microwave-safe pudding bowl.

½ cup (120 g) butter
½ cup (120 g) sugar
2 eggs
1 tsp vanilla extract
1 cup (120 g) self-raising flour
½ tsp baking powder

1 Grease the microwave dish/bowl and place a disc of wax paper in the base.

2 Cream the butter and sugar together until fluffy. Beat in the eggs and vanilla extract. Fold in the flour and baking powder.

3 Spoon into the prepared dish and bake on full power for four minutes (or until a cocktail stick inserted in the center of the cake comes out clean).

4 Leave the cake to stand for 10 minutes before turning out onto a cooling rack.

Chocolate cake
This recipe is for an 7" (18-cm) round microwave cake dish or a 1-quart (l-litre) microwave-safe pudding bowl.

½ cup (120 g) butter
½ cup (120 g) sugar
2 eggs
¾ cup (90 g) self-raising flour
3 tbsp (30 g) cocoa powder
1 tsp baking powder

1 Grease the microwave dish/bowl and place a disc of wax paper in the base.

2 Cream the butter and sugar together until fluffy.

3 Beat in the eggs. Stir in the flour, cocoa and baking powder.

4 Cook on full power for four minutes (or until a cocktail stick inserted in the center comes out clean).

5 Leave the cake to stand for 10 minutes before turning out onto a cooling rack.

Troubleshooting

We all want our cakes to turn out perfectly everytime, but sometimes they don't, even if you're an experienced cook. Here are some of the most common problems and advice on how to avoid them next time.

PROBLEM: The cake sank in the center.

POSSIBLE REASONS:
* The mixture was too runny.
* The oven door was opened too soon and for too long during the cooking process.
* The oven wasn't hot enough.
* The cake was not cooked for long enough.

PROBLEM: The cake burnt.

POSSIBLE REASONS:
* The cake was placed too near to the top of the oven. Always cook in the center of the oven, even with fan ovens.
* The oven was too hot. No matter what it says on the temperature dial, ovens do vary. Next time, cook it on a slightly lower heat.

PROBLEM: The cake seemed very dry.

POSSIBLE REASONS:
* It was overcooked. Reduce the cooking time the next time you make it.
* There wasn't enough liquid in the mixture. If it's virtually impossible to stir the uncooked cake mixture, you need to add a dash more milk or egg.

PROBLEM: The fruit sank.

POSSIBLE REASONS:
* The oven door was opened for too long during cooking.
* There was too much flour in the mixture.

NUMBER AND LETTER CAKES

Thinking of new decorating ideas for birthday cakes year after year can be quite difficult. Creating number and letter shapes out of round or square cakes is very simple to do. The finished cake will always be appreciated by the recipients as it is very personal to them.

Numbers

The easiest way to bake a cake in the shape of a number is to buy or rent a cake pan in the shape of the required number (Fig. a). Most cake decorating and kitchen equipment shops offer this service. To work out how much cake mixture you will need, use the tip given on page 9 for calculating the amount required to fill an unusual shaped pan.

Grease the sides of the pan and line it with a strip of wax paper. If the pan has a base, trace around the pan itself and cut out a piece to lay on the base of the pan. Stand the pan on a baking sheet when cooking so that the heat is evenly distributed along the base of the cake.

If you cannot obtain a number shaped pan, you can cut numbers out of square and round cakes instead (Fig. b). On pages 18–19 you will find a guide to show you how you can cut any number out of round and square cakes.

LEFT *A simple option is to decorate the cake with candies arranged in a number on the top.*

RIGHT *One way to deal with "holes" in letters or numbers is to ignore them and to place a decoration or candles in the spot where a "hole" would normally be.*

Guide to cutting numbers out of square and round cakes.

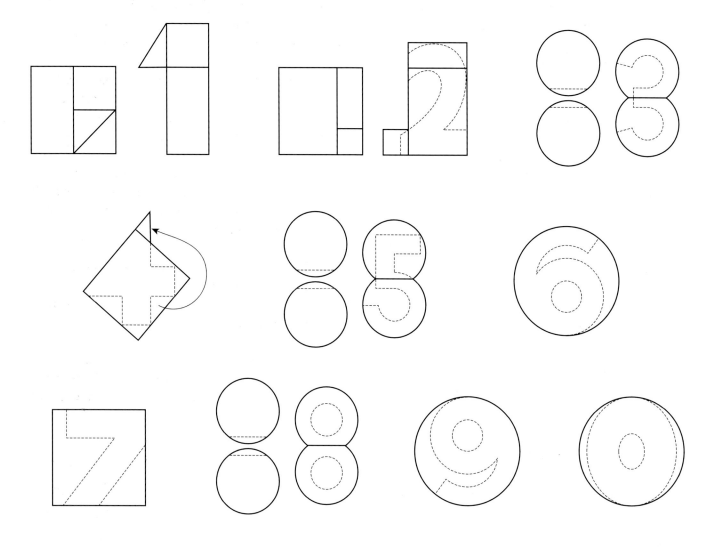

Decorating number-shaped cakes with buttercream

The easiest way to decorate an irregular shaped cake is to cover it with buttercream.

1 Slice the cake into layers as you would a round or square cake.

2 Reassemble it, filling the layers with buttercream. Place on a cakeboard.

3 Spread buttercream around the sides and top (Fig. a) and decorate with candies or other decorations of your choice.

a

Numbers with holes

To decorate a cake in the shape of a number with a hole in it, such as "6", you need to use a slightly different method.

1 Cut the cake into shape and slice into layers.

2 Cut a hole out of the top layer only.

3 Spread a little black buttercream in the center of the next layer. Don't go right to the edge or the black buttercream will "leak" out of the sides when you reassemble the cake.

b

4 Spread your chosen color of buttercream around the outside of the black buttercream on the lower layer and around the outside of the hole in the top layer (Fig. b).

5 Reassemble the cake and spread buttercream around the sides and top of the cake. Pipe or stick sweets around the edges of the cake.

Decorating with fondant

Simple rounded or straight numbers like "0" or "1" can normally be covered all in one step. Numbers with a lot of curved edges and corners, like "3" are trickier.

1 Slice and fill the cake with buttercream and place it in position on the cake board. Spread a thin coating of buttercream around the outside of the cake. This will ensure that the fondant sticks to the cake.

2 Roll out the fondant. Using the baking pan as a template, cut out an outline of the number and place it on top of the cake. Paint a light line of water around the cut edge of the fondant topping.

3 Roll out some more fondant and cut out a long thin strip. The width of the strip should be the same measurement as the height of the cake, including the fondant topping.

4 Roll up the strip like a loose bandage and unroll it around the sides of the cake (Fig. c). To hide the joins, either pipe or crimp along the top edge of the cake (see page 65).

c

Letters

The same decorating techniques that were used for covering numbers can also be used to decorate letter-shaped cakes. You may be able to rent a letter-shaped cake pan from a cake decorating or kitchen shop. Alternatively, you can create your own out of round or square cakes. You can use any leftover bits of cake to make delicious truffles (see page 118).

RIGHT *"T" is a very simple shape to cut out of a square cake.*

Guide for cutting letters out of square and round cakes

BASIC EQUIPMENT

It is not necessary to purchase everything listed here before you can decorate your first cake. A carving knife, rolling pin, small sharp knife, palette knife and paintbrush are the barest essentials. If you enjoy using fondant, it would be worth buying a cake smoother, as using one dramatically improves the finish of the cake. Build up your collection gradually. A plastic workman's toolbox, which you can buy cheaply from a DIY store, is an ideal container for your tools.

TURNTABLE (1) Although not, strictly speaking, essential, once you've used one, you'll wonder what you ever did without it. Cheaper versions are available in plastic.

RULER (2) Not just for measuring; a ruler can also be useful for pressing lines and patterns into fondant.

MEASURING SPOONS (3) A standard set ensures that you use the same quantities each time you make a recipe.

SCISSORS (4) A decent pair of sharp scissors is essential for making piping bags, cutting linings for pans and, sometimes, fondant.

TAPE MEASURE (5) Useful for measuring cakes and boards to ensure that you have rolled out enough fondant.

PIPING NOZZLES OR TIPS (6) A varied selection is always useful and they can double up as small circle cutters. Metal nozzles are more expensive than plastic but are sharper and more accurate.

SMALL DISHES (7) Useful for holding water when modelling; powdered sugar when rolling out fondant. Also ideal when mixing food color into icing.

BAKING PANS (8) An assortment of shapes and sizes is useful.

SIEVE (STRAINER) (9) Vital for sifting flour and powdered sugar. Also a useful tool for making bushes or hair by simply pushing a lump of fondant through the mesh.

DRINKING STRAWS (10) These can be used as tiny circle cutters and are ideal for making eyes. Held at an angle and pressed into fondant, they can also be used for making the scales on snakes, dinosaurs, etc.

COCKTAIL STICKS (11) For adding food color to fondant and for making frills and dotty patterns.

ROLLING PIN (12) A long rolling pin like the one shown will not leave handle dents in the fondant. Tiny ones are also available and are useful for rolling out small quantities of fondant when modelling. If you don't possess a small rolling pin, a paintbrush handle will often do the job just as well.

FONDANT SMOOTHER (13) By using a smoother like an iron and running it over the surface of a covered cake, small bumps and lumps can literally be ironed out. Essential for achieving a smooth finish.

CUTTERS (14) A vast range of shapes is available in both plastic and metal.

COOLING RACK (15) Available in all shapes and sizes and used for cooling cakes.

MIXING AND PUDDING BOWLS (16 and 26) Essential for mixing cake mixture. Useful for mixing colors into icing and baking rounded cakes.

SMALL SHARP KNIFE (17) A small kitchen knife with a sharp, straight blade will become one of your most important pieces of equipment.

CUTTING BOARD (18) For protecting work surfaces.

PAINTBRUSHES (19) A medium brush is good for sticking things with water when modelling and cleaning out piping nozzles. A fine one is needed for adding delicate detail. Sable brushes are best.

SOFT PASTRY BRUSH (20) It is useful to have two brushes– one for dampening or cleaning large areas, the other for brushing away dusty fingerprints or specks of dried fondant icing.

SCALPEL (21) Invaluable when careful cutting is required, such as when scribing around a template.

CARVING KNIFE (22) A long, sharp serrated knife is essential for shaping and slicing cakes.

PALETTE KNIFE (METAL SPATULA) (23) For spreading jam or buttercream, mixing color into larger quantities of royal icing and lifting small bits of fondant.

WOODEN SPOON (24) As well as stirring cake mixture, the handle can be used as a modelling tool.

WAX PAPER (25) Used for lining pans, making piping bags and storing fruit cakes. Can be used in place of tracing paper.

Ribbons

A collection of ribbons is a must if you're going to take up cake decorating. They make fantastic instant decorations (see Christmas bows on page 102).

Often ribbon is placed around the edge of a cake board, particularly on cakes for special occasions. Double-sided tape is probably the best thing to use to secure the ribbon to the edge of the board as it does not bleed through the ribbon or taint the taste of the cake.

Instant decorations

Don't despair if you've left things to the last minute. Candies, crystalized fruits, flowers, store-bought sugar decorations and ribbon can all be used to make colorful instant decorations. Even a paper doily can be used to create an instant dramatic effect (see page 120).

Take a good look around your local cake decorating equipment shop or specialty kitchenware store. They will have many types of decoration in stock—some edible, some not. Your local supermarket is another good source; you should find a range of things including sprinkles, silver cake balls and chocolate leaves. Silk flowers are another great way of decorating a cake in double-quick time (see page 73).

Candles

Try to make candles part of the design. Use colors that tone with the cake. On novelty cakes, it might be possible to stand them in thick, cut-out shapes or balls of fondant so that they tie in with the design. You can even stick the holders into marshmallows, then fix the marshmallows onto the board with dabs of royal icing or buttercream. Be very careful if you're using candles on cakes that use rice paper or silk flower decorations which are flammable. Position the candles well away from the decorations, light for the minimum amount of time and never leave unattended.

Pillars and stands

There are many different styles and designs of pillar. Some plain, some incredibly decorative. Although none of the cake designs in this book actually include pillars, here is a brief look at the basics of what they are and how to use them, in case you decide that you want to adapt one of the cake designs to include pillars.

The pillars have plastic dowels inside them (special plastic rods manufactured to comply with food regulations; available from cake decoration shops). Although the pillars might look sturdy it is the hidden dowels that bear the weight of the cakes above.

Cake stands

Cake stands are an easy way of displaying wedding cakes and are a great idea for the beginner as well as the professional. There are no pillars, dowels or measurements involved. All that is required is the ability to look up your nearest cake decoration shop or bakery in the telephone directory to see where you can rent one.

There are many styles and designs available. They can range from two tiers to six or more. A two-tier stand was used for the Wedding star on page 104.

Using pillars on fondant or buttercream cakes

1 Decide how many pillars you want—usually three or four. Make a template of the top of the cake by drawing around the pan it was baked in onto wax paper.

2 Fold the template in half and half again. Unfold the paper and make a mark on one of the folds, the distance in from the edge of the cake you'd like the pillar to be. Make corresponding marks on the other folds.

3 Place the template on top of the cake and using something like a pin or tip of a scalpel, make a tiny mark through each of the dots onto the surface of the cake (Fig. a). Remove the template.

4 Measure the height of the cake and the height of the pillar and add the two measurements together. Make a mark on one of the cake dowels the same length as that joint measurement.

5 Using a serrated knife, make a little saw mark at that point on the dowel and then bend and snap the unwanted section off.

6 Slot the dowel into one of the marked positions on the cake. Slide the pillar on top. Repeat for all of the other pillars (Fig. b). Because they bear the weight of the cake above, it is essential that the top of the dowel is level with the top of the pillar. If it is lower, the pillar will be squashed down into the cake beneath.

Using pillars on royal-iced cakes

There are various ways of using pillars on a traditional royal-iced fruit cake, but below I have detailed the simplest, quickest method. To prepare the cakes, cover each fruit cake with marzipan and a minimum of three thin coatings of royal icing. Allow each coating to dry thoroughly before applying the next. It is essential that the top of each iced cake is flat and level. Use a small spirit level to check. Fig. c shows a two-tier cake.

When the iced cake has dried, make marks on the cake's surface for the pillars. Scratch a hole into the icing at each of these points using the tip of a scalpel or scriber. The hole needs to be big enough to accommodate a cake dowel. Then follow steps 4 to 6 for Using pillars on fondant or buttercream cakes.

How easy?

All of the cakes in this book can be made successfully by a beginner, but, obviously, there are some cakes that are simpler than others. You will notice that each cake has been allocated a number. This is a quick reference guide to give you a rough idea of how involved the design is and therefore how much time it is likely to take you.

1 Easy

2 Fairly easy

3 Has intricate elements

BUTTERCREAM ICING

Buttercream is probably the easiest type of icing to both make and use. Made from a mixture of butter, powdered sugar and a little water, it can be used to fill and cover cakes, and for piping and making decorations.

Recipe

Making up a batch of buttercream will only take you a few minutes.

ingredients

(Amounts for 1 quantity)

1 cup (250 g) softened butter, preferably unsalted

3½ cups (500 g) powdered sugar

1 tbsp boiled, hot water

1 tsp vanilla extract

1 Beat the butter until soft and fluffy.

2 Add the sugar, water and extract. Beat until pale and creamy.

Different flavors

White or milk chocolate

Stir either 3 oz (90 g) melted white or plain chocolate, or 1 tablespoon cocoa powder mixed to a paste with about 1–2 tablespoons of hot water, into the buttercream.

Coffee

Mix about 1 tablespoon of instant coffee into 1 tablespoon of water and beat into the buttercream.

Flavored extracts

You can use vanilla, peppermint, lemon or almond extract to flavor buttercream. Just add a few drops and mix in.

Coloring buttercream

It is best to use paste colors as they are not as runny as liquid ones. Liquid colors can be used with buttercream but because of their consistency you will only be able to tint the icing lightly. If it starts to get too soggy and out of control, add more powdered sugar.

As buttercream has a naturally creamy color, some colors like pale blue and pale pink will never be quite as true as they would be were the colors being mixed into pure white royal icing. However, if you beat and beat and beat buttercream (and you'll need a food mixer for this otherwise your arm will drop off!) it will eventually turn almost white and will take very pale colors a little better. The other thing to remember when you are adding color is that the shade will deepen as the buttercream sets.

1 Add the color using a cocktail stick (Fig. a).

2 Mix into the buttercream, ensuring that it is blended evenly (Fig. b).

Freezing buttercream

Buttercream freezes extremely well. This quality is exploited in the frozen buttercream transfer cakes on pages 50–51 and 54–55.

If you are covering a cake and find that you have a lot of buttercream left over, it can be placed in a bag or plastic container and frozen until the next baking day comes around. Let it defrost at room temperature for a few hours, then give it a stir. As with all foods, never refreeze buttercream once it has been defrosted.

Another useful fact is that because both sponge cake and buttercream freeze well, you can actually freeze a ready-buttercreamed cake. Protect it with freezer wrap. Defrosting will take anything from 5–12 hours depending upon the room temperature. Condensation will form as it defrosts but avoid the temptation to dab it, the cake will dry naturally. Occasionally, strong colors such as black may run a little.

Filling the cake

Have you ever sliced a cake up, filled it with buttercream, put it back together again and found that none of the layers now seem to fit properly? Here's a little trick to stop that happening.

1 Before you slice the cake into layers, make a buttercream mark down the side of the cake (Fig. c). You can mark it with a knife cut, but I prefer to use buttercream as I tend to lose the cut mark in a flurry of crumbs!

2 Slice your cake into layers and spread buttercream over the top of the base layer. Place the next layer on top of the bottom one – and here's the trick – line the buttercream marks up with each other. If you have a third layer, repeat the procedure, again lining the buttercream marks up (Fig. d).

3 Ensure that the layers are even (Fig. e).

Covering with buttercream

When covering a cake with buttercream, cover the sides first. This allows you to hold the top of the cake steady with your other hand without getting too sticky. Spread the buttercream around the sides and over the top (Fig. f).

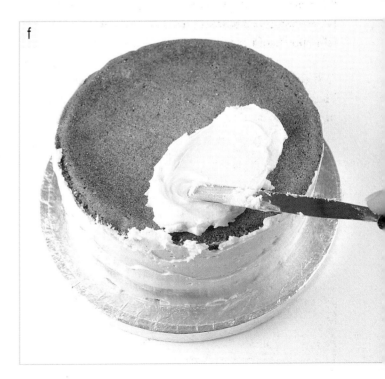

"Setting up" and avoiding crumbs

If you coat your cake with a thin covering of buttercream then place it in the refrigerator for a couple of hours to "set up" before covering it with a second, final coating, you will help yourself in two ways. First, it prevents crumbs from being dragged around the surface of the cake. Second, it stops the cake from moving as you buttercream it. This is especially useful when coating tall cakes such as the Puppet on a string and Candy house (see pages 44–45 and 46–47).

Special effects

There are many different effects you can achieve in buttercream by using different techniques, tools and colors.

Combing

An icing comb is a plastic tool with a serrated edge. As it is run around the outside of a cake, a combed effect is left behind (see Summer flowers on pages 48–49). If it is wiggled as it is moved around the cake, it will produce a zigzag pattern (see Who's looking at you? on pages 58–59).

If you want to experiment with combing but don't have a comb, you can very easily make your own. Cut a rectangle out of an ice cream container lid. Cut a few triangles out of one side and you have a homemade icing comb.

Marbling

By partially mixing a little food color into the buttercream you get a marbled effect—great for making water effects on novelty cakes.

Multicolored swirls and piping

Achieve a dramatic effect by swirling different colors of buttercream onto a cake's surface (see picture below left).

You can also pipe with two or three different colors in the piping bag at the same time (Figs a and b).

Piping

It is very easy to pipe with buttercream provided that the icing is soft enough to flow easily through the piping nozzle but still holds its shape when piped. If it is too stiff, beat in a little more water.

Because piping with buttercream and royal icing is similar, piping and lettering techniques are described fully in the royal icing section on pages 96–100.

Templates

All of the templates on pages 29–31 are shown at 100%.

Baby face (pages 50–51)

Spring blossom (pages 54–55)

Pretty butterflies (pages 38–39)

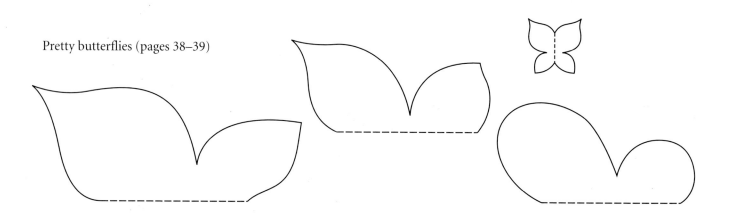

buttercream icing

Buttercream beauty (pages 56–57)

Figure

Border

Celebration cake ❶

The ice cream wafer sticks used here add a pretty pattern to the cake as well as being extremely easy to do. You could substitute chocolate finger cookies if you prefer.

a

b

ingredients

8" (20-cm) round sponge cake (see
    page 10)
2 quantities vanilla buttercream (see
    page 26)
Small, round, sugar-coated chocolate
    candies
Green food color paste
About 54 ice cream wafer fingers
    (approximately 3 packs)

equipment

Carving knife
Palette knife
Cake board
Piping bag (see page 96, but read the
    tip opposite first)
Scissors
No. 3 piping nozzle
1 yd (1 m) lilac ribbon

techniques

Covering a cake with buttercream, page 27
Coloring buttercream, page 26
Making a piping bag, page 97
Piping, page 98

1 Split the cake horizontally two or three times and reassemble it, sandwiching the layers together with buttercream.

2 Place the cake onto the cake board and spread a thick covering of buttercream around the outside of the cake.

3 Place yellow candies—which will form the centers of the flowers—in position on the cake. Make sure there is enough space between them to fit in all the petals.

4 Place six pink or purple candies around each yellow center to form the flowers (Fig. a).

5 To make the leaves, place about a tablespoon of green buttercream in a piping bag. Snip a triangle off the end of the bag. Insert a number 3 piping nozzle and then place 1 tablespoon of green buttercream into the bag. Fold the bag to close.

6 Pipe a leaf between each petal. Simply squeeze some icing out of the end of the bag between two petals. Then release the pressure on the bag and pull away. The icing should fall away forming a tail (Fig. b).

7 Fill the spaces between the flowers with a few additional candies.

8 Press the ice cream wafers around the outside of the cake and finish with a ribbon trim. Use a dab of buttercream to secure the ribbon at the back of the cake.

tip

If you don't have time to do piping or you really don't like doing it, use small bits of angelica or green gum drops instead to make the leaves.

buttercream icing

Silver wedding cake ➊

Sometimes you're in a hurry or perhaps you've been asked to make an important cake but you've never even wielded a rolling pin before let alone a piping bag. Well you're in luck! Most kitchen and cake decorating stores stock all sorts of ready-made decorations. These silver paper rose leaves link beautifully with a silver wedding theme and look lovely and sparkly too. Even better, there's not a piping bag in sight!

ingredients
7" (18-cm) square sponge cake (see page 10)
1 quantity vanilla buttercream (see page 26)
Edible silver balls

equipment
Carving knife
Palette knife
9" (23-cm) square cake board
5"–6" (13–15 cm) diameter bowl
Tweezers (optional; see tip opposite)
About 64 silver paper rose leaves
1 yd (1 m) silver ribbon
Scissors

techniques
Covering a cake with buttercream, page 27

1 Turn the cake upside down. If it won't sit flat on your work surface, turn it back over and slice the top to make it level, then turn it over again.

2 Slice the cake horizontally into two or three layers. Reassemble it, sandwiching the layers together with buttercream.

3 Place the cake on the board and spread buttercream around the outside of the cake.

4 Carefully place a bowl upside down on the top of the iced cake and just as carefully, lift it off. It should have left a circular impression in the icing (Fig. a).

5 Using the impression as a guide, stick a circle of silver balls around the top of the cake (Fig. b).

6 Stick the silver rose leaves around the top edge and base of the cake. Make a ribbon bow and place it in the center. Finally, press a few additional balls into the icing around the cake.

tip
You may find it easier to use a pair of tweezers to handle the silver balls—they can be a bit tricky.

a

b

Teddy bear ❶

This cute teddy is very easy to do. If you don't want to use marzipan for the eyes and ears you could use candies and chocolate buttons for the eyes and nose and small round cookies for the cheeks and ears.

ingredients

8" (20-cm) square sponge cake (see page 10)

1 quantity chocolate buttercream (see page 26)

3½ oz (100 g) golden marzipan

1 tbsp cocoa powder (or brown food color paste)

equipment

Carving knife

Palette knife

12" (30-cm) round cake board

Fork

1 yd (1 m) red ribbon

Scissors

techniques

Covering a cake with buttercream, page 27

Creating effects with buttercream, page 28

Coloring marzipan, page 88

1 Slice about 2" (5 cm) off one side of the square cake to make it rectangular. Place the piece you have cut off against the top of the cake to form a "T" shape.

2 Cut out the teddy shape (see tips below). The head should be rounded, coming into a point at the neck (Fig. a).

3 Slice the cake and fill with buttercream. Place onto the cake board. Spread a thick buttercream coating around the outside of the cake. Use a fork to rough it up to look like fur (Fig. b).

4 Color about 1½ oz (45 g) marzipan brown by kneading in the cocoa powder or food color.

5 Make three ⅛ oz (5 g) dark brown balls for the eyes and nose. Add tiny balls of uncolored marzipan for the highlights. If the highlights won't stick, use a dab of water to hold them in place.

6 Roll out and squash two ½ oz (15 g) balls of uncolored marzipan to make two flattened circles for the cheeks. Place them in position.

7 Add the eyes and the nose. Decorate both cheeks with three tiny flattened brown marzipan dots and add a curved marzipan string for a mouth.

8 To make the ears, roll 1 oz (30 g) brown marzipan and ½ oz (15 g) uncolored marzipan into balls. Place the smaller one on top of the larger one and flatten them both together. Cut the flat disc in half and stick one ear either side of the head.

9 Finish the teddy bear off with a snazzy red bow.

tips

If you are unsure about cutting directly into the cake to make the teddy bear shape, make a template first out of wax paper. Place this on top of the cake and cut around it.

Stand birthday cake candles in their holders in balls of marzipan or regular-sized marshmallows (see page 24). With a dab of water, stick these around the cake board away from the cake (particularly the ribbon bow).

a

b

Pretty butterflies ❶

An elegant yet simple design that would be suitable for Valentine's Day, an anniversary or a birthday. If you don't want to make it heart-shaped, the butterflies work just as well on square and round cakes.

ingredients

5–6 sheets edible rice paper

Edible dusting powders in assorted colors

2 tbsp powdered sugar

7" (18-cm) square sponge cake (see
    page 10)

2 quantities pink buttercream (see
    page 26)

equipment

Scissors

Pencil

Saucer

Wax paper or tracing paper

Carving knife

Palette knife

10" (25-cm) round cake board

techniques

Coloring buttercream, page 26

Covering a cake with buttercream,
    page 27

1 To make the butterflies you can just cut them out freehand or use the templates supplied on page 30. If cutting freehand, simply fold a piece of rice paper in half and cut out half a butterfly shape. If using the templates, make sure that the edge of the template lines up with the rice paper fold. Cut inside the pencil lines (Fig. a). Open out the butterfly and place to one side. Make about 40.

2 To color the butterflies, place some dusting powders on the edge of a saucer and some powdered sugar in the center. Using your finger, mix a little dusting powder with a little powdered sugar and spread onto a butterfly's wings using a light circular motion (see Fig. a, page 57). If the rice paper is rough side up, a textured effect will appear. Color the rice paper on one side only. Decorate all of the butterflies and place to one side.

3 Trace around the heart-shaped cake template on page 67 and cut out. Place the template on top of the cake and cut out the shape (Fig. b).

4 Slice the cake into two or three layers and sandwich the layers together with buttercream. Place the cake on the board and spread a thick covering of buttercream around the top and sides.

5 Gently press the butterflies into the buttercream all over the cake.

tips

You can prepare your butterflies weeks ahead if you wish.

Be very careful if using candles on a cake like this as the rice paper could easily catch fire. If you really want to use candles stick butterflies around the sides of the cake only and place the candles on top.

a

b

Take the train ❶

Incredible though it may seem, there is absolutely no baking involved in this cake—it can all be bought from the supermarket (although you can use your own baked cakes if you wish). The only thing you need to make is some buttercream for sticking the elements together.

ingredients

6 mini chocolate Swiss rolls

1 quantity buttercream (see page 26)

1 large chocolate Swiss roll

1 Battenburg cake (or similar—any
    rectangular chunk of cake will do!)

7 plain, round cookies

2 white chocolate buttons

Assorted small, round, colored candies

1 red jelly bean

About 14 chocolate finger cookies

1 mini jam Swiss roll

2 breadsticks

¼ cup (30 g) flaked coconut

Black and green food color pastes

equipment

10 " (25-cm) square cake board

Carving knife

Palette knife

Fork

techniques

Coloring buttercream, page 26

Creating effects with buttercream,
    page 28

1 Place six mini Swiss rolls in a diagonal line on the cake board. Fix in place with dabs of buttercream.

2 Place the large Swiss roll on top so that it overhangs the rolls at the front. Leave enough room at the other end to stand the Battenburg cake up, so trim the Swiss roll to size if necessary. The roll represents the engine.

3 Stand the Battenburg cake upright on the mini rolls, behind the engine and fix in place with buttercream (Fig. a). The Battenburg cake is the driver's cab.

4 Stick three plain cookies along both sides of the engine to form the wheels. Stick another one on the front of the train ready for the face.

5 To make the face, use two white chocolate buttons and two small round brown candies for the eyes. Use a pink candy for the nose and a red jellybean for the mouth. Stick in place with buttercream (Fig. b).

6 Stick about six chocolate fingers on top of the driver's cab and candies around the edges of the engine and cab.

7 Stick a mini jam roll funnel upright on top of the engine and a breadstick horizontally along each set of wheels.

8 Use about four chocolate fingers to make short sections of track in front of and behind the train. Fix in place with buttercream (Fig. c).

9 Place the coconut into a bowl and mix some black food color into it using a spoon or your fingers. Carefully sprinkle the colored coconut "gravel" between the tracks. (You can leave this step out if you find it too tricky.)

10 Color the leftover buttercream green and spread it around the rest of the board. Use a fork to rough it up a little to resemble grass.

tips

If you're feeling really ambitious you could paint a food color face on a sweet or directly onto the marzipan on the front of the cab to look like the driver.

Stand birthday cake candles in holders in regular-sized marshmallows and press these into the grass, well away from the train.

a

b

c

buttercream icing

Buttercream flowers ❷

This star piping technique is easy to master and produces an interesting texture as well as an attractive design. This cake would be suitable for all sorts of occasions—birthdays, Mother's Day, Easter—to name but a few.

ingredients

7" (18-cm) round sponge cake (see page 10)

2 quantities vanilla buttercream (see page 26)

1 strand uncooked spaghetti or similar

Pink, yellow, green food color pastes

equipment

Carving knife

Palette knife

9" (23-cm) round cake board

Star piping nozzles

Piping bags (see page 96)

Small bowls for mixing colors

techniques

Layering and filling a cake, page 27

Coloring buttercream, page 26

Making a piping bag, page 97

Piping stars, page 98

1 Level the top of the cake and turn it upside down. Split the cake horizontally and fill the layers with buttercream.

2 Place the cake onto the cake board and spread a thin coating of buttercream over the outside of the cake.

3 Using a strand of spaghetti, gently score the outline of the pattern you are going to pipe into the buttercream. If you go wrong, smooth the buttercream over and start again. Draw wiggly lines for the stems and a circle surrounded by petals for the flowers (Fig. a). These lines will be hidden by the piping.

4 Place a star nozzle into a piping bag. Put about a tablespoon of pink icing into the bag and fold the end of the bag to close it.

5 Pipe a star on the edge of one of the flower centers. Just squeeze a bit of icing out of the end of the nozzle, release the pressure and pull the bag upward, away from the cake. Pipe a ring of stars around the outside of one of the flower centers then fill in the middle. Repeat on the other two flower centers (Fig. b).

6 Repeat the procedure on the flower petals using yellow buttercream. Then pipe and fill in the stems and the leaves with green. Finally, fill in the outside of the cake using uncolored buttercream.

7 To decorate the board, pipe a line of green stars around the base of the cake. Follow this with a ring of uncolored buttercream, then a line of pink.

8 To finish, pipe a few single pink stars over the cake.

tip

This cake can be decorated and then frozen. Store it carefully in the freezer to avoid damage and defrost gently at room temperature for 6–8 hours.

a   b

Puppet on a string ❷

Now admit it, you never knew a breadstick could be this useful did you? Here they make great handles for dangling a puppet on a string.

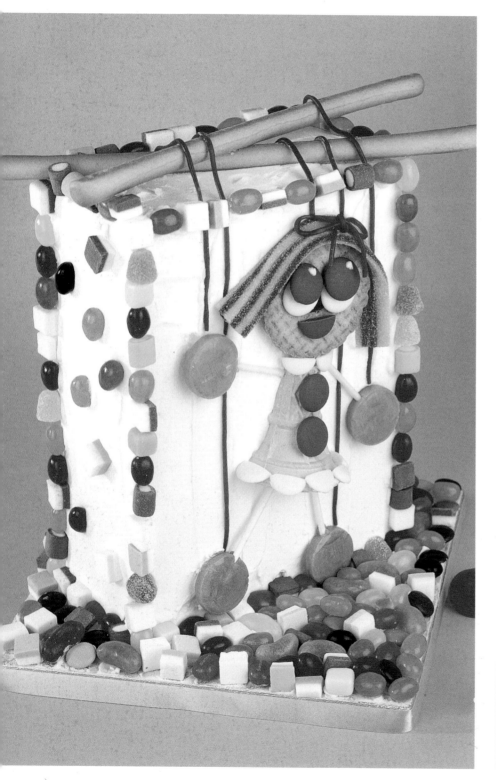

ingredients

8" (20-cm) square sponge cake (see page 10)

1 quantity vanilla buttercream (see page 26)

2 breadsticks

4 lollipops

Liquorice strings

1 ice cream cone

1 round cookie

2 strands of fruit leather for hair

White and milk chocolate buttons

Assorted candies for decorating cake and board

equipment

Carving knife

8" (20-cm) square cake board

Palette knife

Scissors

Small sharp knife

techniques

Covering cake with buttercream, page 27

"Setting up," page 28

tips

To make a boy puppet use a second round cookie to make a body instead of the dress. Decorate with a couple of chocolate buttons. Give him shorter hair and leave the bow off.

Either stand birthday cake candles in holders on the top of the cake or stand the holders in marshmallows and stick them onto the cake board with buttercream.

1 Slice about 2" (5 cm) off one side of the square cake to form an 8" × 6" (20 × 15 cm) rectangle.

2 Stand the cake upright on one of the shorter sides. Use what was originally the flat base of the cake to form a smooth front.

3 If you want to fill the cake with buttercream, slice the cake horizontally into two or three layers and reassemble it with buttercream filling.

4 Stand the cake diagonally on the cake board and spread buttercream over the sides and top.

5 If you have time, place the cake in the fridge for about an hour so that the buttercream can harden. Spread another coating of buttercream over the outside of the cake when you remove it from the fridge so that the candies have something to stick to.

6 Lay two crossed breadsticks on top of the cake. Use dabs of butter-cream to hold them in place.

7 Press two lollipops into the lower part of the cake for the legs.

8 Cut two pieces of liquorice strings, about 10" (25 cm) long, for the strings. Press them into the cake so that they run from a lollipop foot, up the cake and over the top of the breadsticks. Trim if necessary and press the ends into the buttercream on top of the cake (Fig. a).

9 Carefully cut the pointed end off an ice cream cone and slice the cone in half. Place it over the top of the legs to form a dress. Add a cookie for the head Fig. b).

10 Add two more lollipops for arms and licorice strings leading from the arms and head to the breadsticks.

11 Use a couple strips of fruit leather to make the hair, pressing them gently into the buttercream so that they stay in place.

12 Use two white and two milk chocolate buttons for the eyes. Stick them onto the cookie face with dabs of buttercream. Add a tiny buttercream dot for a highlight (Fig. c).

13 For the mouth, cut a milk chocolate button in half and stick in place. Cut four white chocolate buttons in half. Use two to make the collar and five to make a frill around the bottom of the dress. Stick two milk chocolate buttons on the front of the dress. Make a licorice string bow and stick it on top of the head.

14 Smear the cake board with buttercream and press candies all around the outside edges of the cake and over the cake board.

a

b

c

Candy house ❷

Just watch your child's face light up with delight when this fairy tale house arrives on the table. It may look terribly complicated at first glance but in fact it is very easy to assemble. If you are planning to incorporate candles into the design, please read the tip below before you start.

ingredients

10" (25-cm) square sponge cake (see page 10)

1 quantity buttercream (see page 26; color 4 tbsp green for the grass, flavor the rest with chocolate)

Green food color paste

Milk and white chocolate finger cookies

3 thin slices Battenburg cake or square cookies

At least 15 ice cream wafers

Assorted small candies and mini marshmallows for brickwork

1 mini Swiss roll

Multicolored candies for gravel

Coconut mushrooms

equipment

Carving knife

Palette knife

12" (30-cm) round cake board

Fork

tip

To incorporate candles safely, make sure that the house is positioned at the back of the cake board and only use the chocolate finger fencing around the back and sides of the house. Stick the candles into holders and insert the holders into regular-sized marshmallows. Stand the candles around the edge of the board as far away from the house as possible.

1 If your cake has a very rounded top, slice a bit off to level it, then cut the entire cake in half diagonally.

2 Place the two triangular halves on top of each other. Slice a small triangle off each end (Fig. a).

3 Sandwich the layers together with buttercream. Stand the cake upright on the board and spread a thin coating of buttercream over the outside of the cake (Fig. b). If you have time, place the cake in the refrigerator for an hour.

4 Spread a second, thicker layer of buttercream over the outside of the cake. This will act as glue for the decorations.

5 Place four milk chocolate fingers upright in the center to make a door. Press three thin slices of Battenburg cake or square cookies in position for the windows. Add a couple of white chocolate fingers for steps and window ledges.

6 Then, starting from the bottom, stick a line of overlapping wafers up both sides of the roof (Fig. c). Press one ice cream wafer over the door to make a porch.

7 Fill in the brickwork by pressing candies or mini marshmallows into the buttercream around the house. If you want to save a bit of time and use less candy, leave the back of the house plain, covered with buttercream only.

8 To make the chimney, slice a small diagonal section off a mini Swiss roll. Stick it on the roof with a blob of buttercream and add a small candy for the chimney flue.

9 Stick a line of candies along the roof ridge and a candy for a doorknob. Decorate the roof with a few more candies if you wish. Again, use buttercream as glue.

10 Spread the green buttercream around the cake board. Use a fork to rough up the icing to make it look like grass.

11 To make the fencing, cut about 15 white chocolate fingers in half and stand them upright in the grass all around the house.

12 Sprinkle multicolored candy in front of the door to make a path.

13 Place a few extra candies or coconut mushrooms in the garden.

Summer flowers ❷

All the piping on this cake was done using a number 4 piping nozzle which has
a large round hole in the end. If you don't have one, you can achieve a similar
effect by making a piping bag, filling it and snipping a tiny triangle off the end.

ingredients

2 quantities buttercream (see page 26)

6" (15-cm round sponge cake
 (see page 10)

Yellow, pink, green food color pastes

equipment

Piping bags (see page 96)

No. 4 piping nozzle

Wax paper

Carving knife

Palette knife

8" (20-cm) round cake board

Small bowls for mixing colors

Serrated icing comb (optional)

techniques

Making a piping bag, page 97

Filling and covering a cake with buttercream,
 page 27

Coloring buttercream, page 26

"Setting up," page 28

Combing a cake, page 28

a

b

c

1 Place about 2 tablespoons of buttercream in a piping bag fitted with the number 4 piping nozzle. Pipe five large dots onto wax paper in a flower formation (Fig. a). Make about 30 and leave to set in the fridge for a few hours.

2 In the meantime, prepare the cake. Split the cake into two or three layers and reassemble it, filling the layers with buttercream. Color all but 5 tablespoons of the rest of the buttercream yellow.

3 Place the cake on the board and spread a thin coating of yellow buttercream all over the outside of the cake. Put in the fridge for an hour or so to "set up". This will stop crumbs from getting caught up in the icing and spoiling the finish of the cake later.

4 When ready, spread a thicker coating of yellow buttercream over the sides. Run a serrated icing comb around the sides of the cake (optional).

5 Spread additional yellow buttercream over the top of the cake and run the icing comb over it (optional; Fig. b).

6 Using a palette knife, spread a thin coating of yellow buttercream over the cake board (Fig. c).

7 When the flowers are set, carefully lift them off the wax paper with a knife and stick around the top edge of the cake with a blob of buttercream. Stick a cluster of three in the center and the rest around the base of the cake.

8 Color about a tablespoon of buttercream pink and place in a piping bag with the number 4 piping nozzle. Fold the bag to close. Pipe five dots in the center of each flower. Wash the nozzle.

9 Color the rest of the buttercream green and place in another piping bag with the number 4 piping nozzle. To pipe the leaves between the flowers, simply squeeze the bag, release the pressure and pull away. The icing will fall away, leaving a tapering tail behind.

variation

This version still conveys a feeling of freshness even though there are fewer flowers on it. There is no combing involved and just three flowers in the center. Leaves were piped around the top and base of the cake. Pink dots, in groups of three, were then piped both among the leaves and around the top and sides of the cake.

Baby face ❷

This technique called "frozen buttercream transfer" is a simple way to put pictures on top of cakes. Note that you will need to have a freezer in order to make the transfer. This would make a cute christening cake or a first birthday cake.

ingredients

2 quantities buttercream (see page 26)

Black, pink, yellow, blue food color pastes

6" (15-cm) square sponge cake (see page 10)

Small gum drops

equipment

Pencil

Wax paper or tracing paper

Scissors

2 thin cake boards or pieces of card (bigger than the design)

Plastic wrap, wax paper

Adhesive tape

Piping bags (see page 96)

No. 2 piping nozzle

Small bowls for mixing colors

Dressmaker's pin

Carving knife

Palette knife

techniques

Making a piping bag, page 97

Coloring buttercream, page 26

Piping, page 98

Filling and covering a cake with buttercream, page 27

1 Trace the baby design on page 29 onto wax paper or tracing paper. If you want to make a cake of a different size, use a photocopier to alter the size of the design.

2 Place the design onto a thin cake board and put a sheet of plastic wrap over the top. Use a tiny bit of tape at the edges to hold it in place if you wish.

3 Place about a tablespoon of black buttercream into a piping bag fitted with a number 2 piping nozzle. Trace the picture and fill in the baby's mouth (see Fig. a page 55).

4 Place some pink buttercream in a piping bag. Close the end and snip a tiny triangle off the pointed end. Fill in the outline of the picture (see Fig. b page 55). Refer to the photograph opposite to help you put the colors in the right places.

5 Repeat the procedure with the blue and yellow buttercream and fill in the background of the picture with uncolored buttercream.

6 When you have finished the picture, carefully remove the tape from the corners and gently lay a second sheet of plastic wrap over the top of the design.

7 Place a second thin cake board on top of the pile and carefully turn the layers over. Gently press down and squash the boards together.

8 Remove what is now the top board and the traced design. Using your finger, gently rub over the plastic wrap in a circular motion to get rid of the piping marks (Fig. a). Prick any air bubbles with a pin.

9 When you have finished, place the second cake board back on top of the picture and place in the freezer for at least an hour.

10 Cut the cake in half horizontally and sandwich the layers together with buttercream. Place the cake onto the cake board and spread a smooth covering of buttercream over the top and sides of the cake.

11 When frozen, remove the board and plastic wrap from the back of the design.

12 Carefully lift the design by the edges of the plastic wrap and lay the buttercreamed side on top of the cake. Peel off the plastic wrap (Fig. b).

13 Spread buttercream over the cakeboard and press a line of gum drops around the edges of the cake. Place a few drops in the corners and at the sides of the cake, and scatter some on the board.

a

b

Bouquet of hyacinths ❷

This cake is a perfect demonstration of how limiting the number of colors on a cake can actually enhance the design. If in doubt, keep it simple. Practice piping the stars a few times first before you attempt the real thing.

buttercream icing

ingredients

6" (15-cm) round sponge cake (see
    page 10)
2 quantities buttercream (see page 26)
Green, purple, blue food color pastes

equipment

Carving knife
Palette knife
8" (20-cm) round cake board
No. 4 piping nozzle
Scissors
Piping bags (see page 96)
Small bowls for mixing colors
Star piping nozzle

techniques

Filling and covering a cake with
    buttercream, page 27
Coloring buttercream, page 26
Making a piping bag, page 97
Piping stars, page 98

1 Level the top of the cake and split it horizontally into two or three layers. Reassemble the cake, filling the layers with buttercream.

2 Place the cake on the cake board and spread buttercream around the top and sides.

3 Place the number 4 piping nozzle in a piping bag. Color about 2 tablespoons of buttercream green and place in the bag. Fold over the end of the bag to close it and pipe lines for the stems and leaves around the sides of the cake (Fig. a). Pipe a cluster of stems and leaves on top of the cake.

4 Color about 2 tablespoons of buttercream purple and place in a bag fitted with the star piping nozzle. Pipe a line of stars either side of one of the stems on top of the cake (Fig. b). Repeat on alternate flower stems all around the sides of the cake.

5 When you have piped all of the purple flowers, pipe a line of stars around the top edge of the cake.

variation

You can use the same star piping technique to make simple daisy flowers too. Pipe a central yellow star, then pipe five or six pink ones around the outside.

6 Wash and dry the star piping nozzle and place into a second piping bag. Color about 2 tablespoons of buttercream blue and place into the bag. Pipe the remaining flowers and ring on top of cake (Fig. c).

a

b

c

Spring blossom ❷

This cake is made using the same frozen transfer method as Baby face (see page 50), but piping and combing techniques are also used (see tip below).

ingredients

2 quantities buttercream (see page 26)

Black, yellow, pink, green, brown food
  color pastes

7" (18-cm) round sponge cake (see
  page 10)

equipment

Pencil

Wax paper or tracing paper

Scissors

2 thin cake boards or pieces of card
  (bigger than the design)

Plastic wrap, wax paper

Adhesive tape

Piping bags (see page 96)

No. 2 and star piping nozzles

Small bowls for mixing colors

Dressmaker's pin

Carving knife

Palette knife

Serrated icing comb (optional)

techniques

Coloring buttercream, page 26

Making a piping bag, page 97

Piping, page 98

Filling and covering a cake with
  buttercream, page 27

Combing, page 28

1 Trace the flower design on page 30 onto wax paper or tracing paper. If you want to make a cake of a different size, alter the size of the design using a photocopier.

2 Place the design onto a thin cake board and place a sheet of plastic wrap over the top. Use a tiny bit of tape at the edges to hold it in place.

3 Place about a tablespoon of black buttercream into a piping bag fitted with a number 2 piping nozzle. Pipe over the outline of the picture (Fig. a).

4 Place some yellow buttercream in a piping bag. Close and snip a tiny triangle off the end. Fill in the design using the appropriate colors (Fig. b). Use uncolored buttercream for the background.

5 Carefully remove the tape from the corners and gently lay a second sheet of plastic wrap over the top of the design. Place a second thin cake board on top of the pile and carefully turn the layers over. Gently press down and squash the boards together.

6 Remove what are now the top board and the traced design. Using your finger, gently rub the plastic wrap in a circular motion to get rid of the piping marks (see Fig. a page 51). Use a pin to prick any air bubbles that might develop.

7 Place the second cake board back on top and put in the freezer for at least an hour.

8 Cut the cake in half horizontally and sandwich the layers together with buttercream. Place the cake onto the cake board and spread quite a thick coating of buttercream over the sides of the cake. If you wish, run an icing comb around the outside of the cake to make a pattern (see Fig. b page 49). Spread a thin buttercream coating over the top of the cake.

9 When the design has frozen, take it out of the freezer and remove the top board and sheet of plastic wrap from the back of the design.

10 Carefully lift the design by the edges of the film and lay the buttercreamed side on top of the cake. Peel off the plastic wrap (see Fig. b page 51).

11 Pipe a line of shells around the top and bottom edges of the cake and pipe a few pink stars on the side if you wish. You could use sweets instead if you prefer.

tip

To simplify this design, stick candies around the edges of the cake instead of piping and combing.

Buttercream beauty ③

This cake may look intricate, but it's actually very easy to put together. The design is simply cut out of rice paper and slotted into the buttercream covering. The decorations can be made weeks in advance.

buttercream icing.

ingredients

1 pack edible rice paper

Edible blue and pink dusting powder

2 tbsp powdered sugar

8" (20-cm) round sponge cake (see page 10)

2 quantities buttercream (see page 26)

equipment

Pencil

Scissors

Saucers

Paintbrush

Carving knife

Palette knife

10" (25-cm) round cake board

Tweezers

tips

To save time you could use just four border sections around both the top and base.

Be careful with candles on this design because the rice paper could catch fire. If you do use them, place securely in candle holders on top of the cake, away from any rice paper twirls and blow them out as soon as possible.

1 With the smooth side of the rice paper facing up, lightly trace over the figure templates on page 31 with a pencil. Cut out just inside the pencil lines.

2 Fold a piece of rice paper in half and line the folded edge up to the edge of the border template. Trace and cut out a border. Open it out and cut out inside the pencil lines. Keep the heart shape from the middle. Make 16.

3 Tip a little blue and pink dusting powder onto a saucer. Place a little powdered sugar in the center. Using your finger, rub some dust into some powdered sugar and then onto the rice paper (smooth side up). Use a light circular motion (Fig. a). Just color along the edge of each piece of rice paper. When coloring the border sections, color eight pink, the rest blue. Also color all the cut out hearts and the shapes for the figure.

4 Color two rice paper rectangles about 4" × 2" (10 × 5 cm); one blue and the other pink. Cut these into thin strips. Wind the strips around a paintbrush handle to curl them (Fig. b). When finished, place all the rice paper sections to one side and prepare the cake.

5 Level the top of the cake and turn it upside down so the base becomes the top. Slice it two or three times horizontally and fill the layers with buttercream.

6 Place the cake onto the cake board and spread buttercream around the top and sides.

7 Insert the rice paper decorations as soon as you've finished coating the cake so that they stick securely. Using the tweezers, place the main dress section in position and poke the neck section into the buttercream to hold it in place. Insert the two petticoat sections and foot beneath it. Then add the two arms and the bonnet pieces.

8 Place two blue and two pink edging sections alternatively around the edge of the cake. Position another ring of four in front of them. Repeat around the base of the cake. Place the cut-out hearts around the border so that they hide the joins.

9 Stick some of the rice paper twirls on top of the cake and the rest into the sides.

a

b

Who's looking at you? ③

The combed effect used on the sides and lid of the box make it look as though it's made of wicker. If you find the prospect of combing a bit daunting, cover the box with smooth buttercream and decorate with a few candies instead.

ingredients

6" (15-cm) square sponge cake (see page 10)
2 quantities vanilla buttercream (see page 26)
Blue and black food color pastes
1 oz (30 g) white fondant or two white marshmallows (see tips below)
½ oz (15 g) black fondant or two chocolate buttons

equipment

Carving knife
Palette knife
8" (20-cm) square cake board
Serrated icing comb (optional)
Piping bag (see page 96)
Star piping nozzle (optional)
6" (15-cm) thin square cake board
Scissors
1 yd (1 m) ribbon

techniques

Filling and covering a cake with buttercream, page 27
Coloring buttercream, page 26
Combing, page 28

1 Level the top of the cake and turn it upside down. Slice it horizontally two or three times. Reassemble the cake, filling the layers with buttercream and place the cake on the board.

2 Color about half of the buttercream pale blue. Spread a thin covering over the sides of the cake. If possible, place the cake in the fridge for about an hour.

3 Remove the cake from the fridge and spread a thicker layer of blue buttercream over the sides.

4 Holding the serrated edge of the comb vertically, run it along the sides of the cake, wiggling it slightly as you go to make the wavy pattern (Fig. a). Color about 3 tablespoons of the buttercream black. Spread this over the top of the cake.

5 Place about 2 tablespoons of uncolored buttercream into a piping bag fitted with the star nozzle. Pipe shells around the edges of the cake.

6 Make two white fondant balls for the eyes. Stick on two black fondant discs and two tiny white balls for highlights with water. Place the eyes onto the top of the cake (Fig. b).

7 To make the lid, spread pale blue buttercream over the thin cake board and use the serrated comb to make a wiggly pattern.

8 Place the lid in position on the cake and pipe around the edges.

9 To finish off, make a jaunty-looking bow and stick it on the top of the cake with a small blob of buttercream.

tips

Another way to make eyes is to stick a chocolate button onto a white marshmallow and add a dot of vanilla buttercream as a highlight.

If you want to put candles on this cake, position the cake as far back on the board as you can. Stand the candles in either fondant balls or marshmallows on the board at the front. Make sure that the tail of the ribbon is not dangling too close to any of the candles.

a

b

FONDANT

Basically, fondant is an edible form of modelling clay. Sometimes called sugarpaste or ready-to-roll icing, it is simple to make and easy to use. It is also available ready-made from supermarkets and cake-decorating shops.

Recipe

There is a slight risk of salmonella from using raw egg (see note page 4). If you prefer, you can use dried egg white. Refer to the instructions on the packet for mixing it up.

ingredients

(Amounts for 1 quantity)

3½ cups (500 g) powdered sugar

1 egg white (or equivalent amount of dried egg white, reconstituted)

2 tbsp (30 ml) liquid glucose (available from drug stores, some supermarkets and cake decorating equipment stores)

1 Place the sugar into a bowl. Make a well in the center.

2 Tip the egg white and glucose into the well and stir in using a wooden spoon.

3 Finish binding the icing together using your hands. Knead until all the sugar is incorporated and the icing feels silky and smooth.

4 Double wrap in two small plastic food bags to prevent it drying out. It can be used right away and does not require refrigeration. Use within a week.

Using fondant

Fondant will harden as it is exposed to air so if you open a packet and just use a bit, rewrap what's leftover in a small plastic food bag to prevent it drying out. Keep unused bags of fondant in a plastic container. It does not need to be kept in the fridge.

When you are rolling it out, always roll it on powdered sugar never flour or cornflour. Keep a bowl of powdered sugar handy to keep your fingers from getting sticky. Don't worry about getting your creation "dusty" with the sugar. Simply brush marks away with a soft, damp paintbrush at the end.

When you are making shapes, you can use water to stick the bits together. Never soak the fondant; apply just a dab with a soft paintbrush to make the surface of the fondant tacky. Try to avoid getting drips of water on the fondant. They will dissolve the surface, leaving an unsightly watermark behind.

QUANTITY GUIDE

The amount of fondant you would use to coat a cake can vary depending upon how thick you like your icing to be. Here is a guide to give you a rough idea.

Round cake	6" (1cm)	7" (18cm)	8" (20cm)	9" (23cm)	10" (25cm)	11" (28cm)	12" (30cm)	
Square cake		6" (15cm)	7" (18cm)	8" (20cm)	9" (23cm)	10" (25cm)	11" (28cm)	12" (30cm)
Fondant	1lb (500g)	1lb 5oz (650g)	1lb 10oz (800g)	2lb (900g)	2lb 8oz (1.1kg)	3lb (1.4kg)	3lb 8oz (1.6kg)	4lb (1.8kg)

Covering a cake with fondant

Before covering with fondant, a sponge cake should be completely covered on the outside with either a coating of buttercream (see page 27) or jam. This will hold the fondant in place.

If you are using a fruit cake, it should first be covered with a layer of marzipan (see page 85). When done, brush the surface of the marzipan with alcohol or cooled, boiled water. This will make it tacky so that the fondant will adhere to it.

1 Dust your work surface with powdered sugar to keep the fondant from sticking. Knead the fondant until it feels soft and pliable.

2 Roll it out to a thickness of about ¼" (6 mm). Don't roll it too thinly or it will show up any irregularities in the cake's surface.

3 Lift the fondant and place over the top of the cake. You can either do this by sliding your hands—palms flat and facing upward underneath the fondant—or with a rolling pin (Fig. a).

4 Starting with the top, to try to avoid air getting trapped underneath, smooth the icing into position. A fondant smoother is useful here to iron out lumps and bumps (Fig. b). If you do get an air bubble, prick it with a dressmaker's pin.

5 Cut away the excess icing from around the base (Fig. c).

BELOW *This cake is a variation on Hearts and ribbons on page 76. Cover the cake and press the heart pattern into the icing. Using about 2 yd (2 m) of ribbon, pass it over the cake and tie under the cake board. Bring the ends back up and tie into a bow on top of the cake.*

Covering cake boards with fondant

Covering the exposed cake board around the base of the cake can often neaten a design. Here are three ways of doing this.

All-in-one
This is the easiest method of covering a board.

1 Lightly moisten the entire board with water and begin to roll out a ball of fondant on your work surface.

2 Lift and place the icing onto the cake board and roll it up to and over the edges of the board (Fig. a). Trim and neaten the edges. The covered cake can now be placed on top.

BELOW *The board for this cake, Frosted flowers (see page 72), was covered using the bandage method.*

The bandage method
This is done after the cake itself has been covered and is in position on the board.

1 Moisten the exposed cake board with a little water.

2 Measure the circumference of the cake and cut out a long, thin fondant strip, a bit longer than that measurement and wider than the exposed board.

3 Slide a knife along under the icing to ensure that it's not stuck to the work surface and roll the icing up like a loose bandage.

4 Starting from the back, unwind the bandage around the board (Fig. b). Trim and neaten the joint and edges.

Using four strips
This is a useful way to cover the board around a square or rectangular cake.

1 Moisten the cake board with a little water.

2 Thinly roll out the fondant and cut out four strips each slightly longer and wider than the exposed sides of the cake board.

3 Lay one strip along each side of the cake. Make a diagonal cut from the edge of the board to the edge of the cake at each corner and peel away the excess icing (Fig. c).

4 The fondant should now form a neat joint at each corner. Trim and neaten the edges.

Coloring fondant

Ready-colored fondant can be bought from cake decorating shops and some supermarkets, but it is easy to color your own. It is best to use paste or gel colors rather than liquid ones. The pastes are thicker and won't make the icing soggy.

1 Apply dabs of food color paste with a cocktail stick (Fig. d).

2 Knead the color in until all of the fondant is an even color (Fig. e).

As well as using food color, you also can knead different colors of fondant together to get different shades, for example you can mix white with black to make grey. For a flat matte color, knead until all the color is mixed in and no streaks are visible.

Different effects with color

Woodgrain effect
Achieving a woodgrain effect is simple and, like marbling (see page 64), it can be done in two ways.

1 Roll some white fondant into a sausage shape and apply some streaks of brown food color (Fig. f) or bits of brown fondant.

2 Fold the fondant in half and roll it into a sausage again. Keep repeating this rolling and folding process and you will see a woodgrain effect appear (Fig. g).

3 Stop before it becomes a solid color and roll the fondant out. If you go too far, add some bits of white fondant and repeat the process.

Marbling

You can either apply a few dabs of food color and only partially knead it in or you can use two different colors of fondant. This method is shown below (Fig. a).

1 Take a lump of white fondant and a smaller ball of the appropriate vein color. Break the smaller lump into pieces and press onto the white.

2 Carefully roll and knead the two together until you see a marbled effect occurring. If you go too far and it all turns one color, reverse the process by adding a bit more white.

3 If you are using black and white fondant like this, then you can pull small bits off and roll them into balls. They make excellent icing pebbles or rocks and can even be used as candle holders.

Multicolored effects

Another easy effect can be achieved by breaking three or four different colors of fondant into lumps, then lightly press and roll them together (Fig. b). Useful if you're putting together a groovy disco or party cake!

Painting on fondant

If possible, leave the cake to harden overnight before painting on it. This will make the surface of the cake less prone to dents if you lean on it. You must only use food colors for painting.

1 Brush the surface of the cake with a pastry brush to get rid of any powdered sugar which might cause the color to bleed.

2 Paint a light outline on the cake first using some watered down food color, then fill it in.

3 Use the food color like watercolor paints, mixing them in a palette to get different shades (Fig. c). If you want to paint a black outline around the images, do this after you have painted the middle. If you paint the black outlines first, the black will bleed into the central color.

4 If you make a mistake, gently dab and break up the error with a soft paintbrush dipped into clean water. Wipe away the mistake with a clean, damp cloth.

Easy fondant effects

Crimping

Crimping tools are available from all cake decorating shops. Inexpensive and easy to use, they are a simple and quick way to give your fondant cakes neat, decorative edges. (See the "letter A" cake on page 17 and the "number 3" cake on page 19).

1 Place the crimper on the edge of the cake, then squeeze firmly and release (Fig. d).

2 The crimper pinches the icing, leaving behind a pattern (Fig. e).

Twisting strands

If you're not keen on piping, a simple, effective edging can be made by twisting a thin fondant strand and laying it around the top or base of a cake (Fig. f). Use dabs of water to hold it in place.

Quilting and embossing

A quilted effect can be made by using a ruler to press lines into the fondant. You can also achieve an embossed effect by pressing things into the fondant. Cake decorating shops sell decorative stamps especially designed for this, but you can also use cutters to make a similar effect (see Hearts and ribbons on page 76).

Fondant cutters

There are all sorts of cutters available from cake decorating and kitchen shops which you can use to cut out a variety of patterns and shapes, including flowers and leaves.

The tiny cutters in the foreground of this picture below are called plunge cutters. They cut out tiny flower shapes. They have a small plunger inside which helps expel the flower so you can press it directly onto the cake.

Lettering

It is also possible to buy sets of alphabet cutters so you can cut out letters and stick words onto the top of your cake. You can also use letter cutters as embossers and press them into the iced cake to make words.

Modelling with fondant

a

b

Simple figures

If you were to pull a fondant figure apart you would see that the shapes of the components are very simple—usually a collection of cone, ball and sausage shapes (Fig. a). Make the components as you go along, otherwise the pieces may crack when you come to assemble the figure.

It is easier to make lying or sitting figures rather than standing ones. If the figure seems a bit wobbly, poke a short length of uncooked spaghetti inside to act as a support. Use light dabs of water to stick the components of the body together.

Plaques

There are a couple of advantages to using decorated plaques on a cake. First; they can be made weeks in advance. Second; if you are a little scared about piping a message directly onto a cake, you can pipe it onto a plaque first then place the plaque onto the cake. If you make a mistake on a plaque, it only takes a few minutes to make another one.

1 Cut out a piece of fondant to the desired shape. Leave to dry.

2 The plaque can be decorated in whatever manner you like—it can be piped, painted on or decorated with candies.

Simple roses

Cakes decorated with fondant flowers look beautiful, but they are quite tricky to make and take a lot of practice. However, simple roses are very easy to make and look effective and elegant (Fig. b). There is an even simpler rose shown on page 118, which can be made out of fondant as well.

1 Make a small fondant cone shape. Pinch one side to make a flap and wind around the outside of the cone.

2 Make two small, flat petals and stick around the center, on the lower part of the petal, with dabs of water.

3 Make three more petal shapes and stick around the outside of the rose. The petals should overlap slightly. Tweak the tips of the petals and cut off any excess from the base. Cut simple leaf shapes out of green fondant. Press the back of a knife into the icing to create veins.

Templates

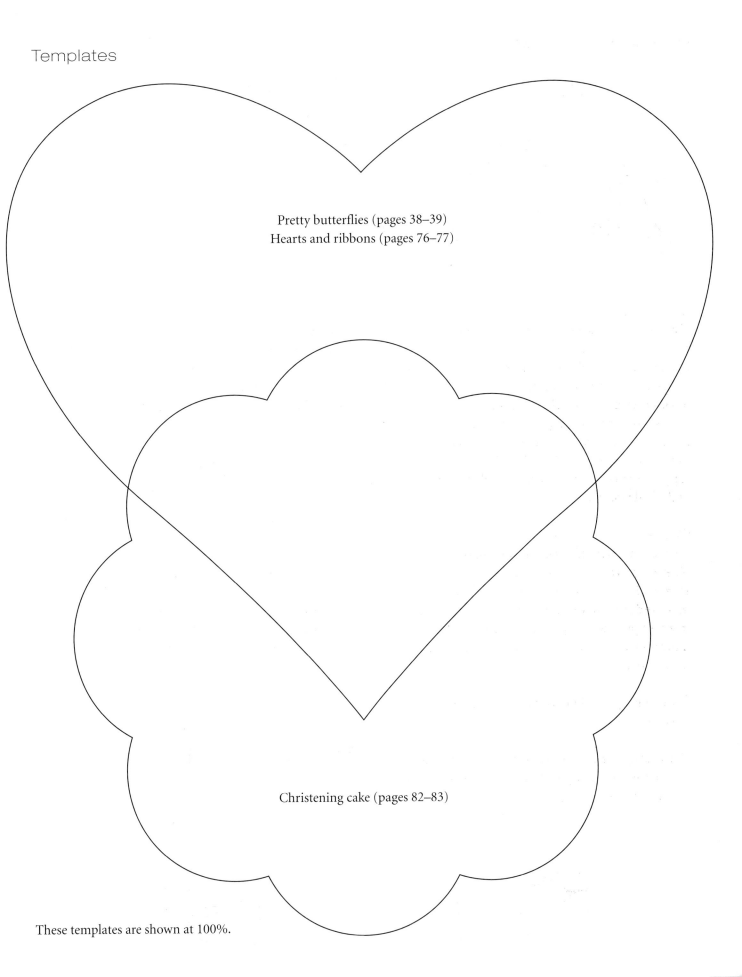

Pretty butterflies (pages 38–39)
Hearts and ribbons (pages 76–77)

Christening cake (pages 82–83)

These templates are shown at 100%.

Party balloons ❶

A versatile cake that is suitable for all sorts of happy occasions—birthdays, good-bye parties, a new house, passing exams—basically any celebration.

ingredients

6" (15-cm) round sponge cake (see page 10)
1 quantity buttercream (see page 26)
Powdered sugar for rolling out
1 lb 2 oz (500 g) white fondant
1 oz (30 g) red fondant
1 oz (30 g) yellow fondant
1 oz (30 g) blue fondant
1 oz (30 g) green fondant
Black food color
Small, round colored chocolate candies

equipment

Carving knife
Palette knife
8" (20-cm) round cake board
Rolling pin
Paintbrush
Fondant smoother (optional)
Small sharp knife
Piping bag (see page 96; also see tip opposite)
No. 1 piping nozzle (see tip opposite)

techniques

Filling and covering a cake with buttercream, page 27
Coloring fondant, page 63
Covering a cake with fondant, page 61

1 Level the cake and turn it upside down. Slice it into two or three layers, fill the layers with buttercream and reassemble.

2 Place the cake onto the cake board and spread buttercream around the sides and top of the cake.

3 Dust your work surface with powdered and knead and roll out the white fondant to a thickness of about ¾" (2 cm).

4 Roll each of the four fondant colors into tiny balls and stick onto the white, using very light dabs of water.

5 Roll over the entire slab of icing (Fig. a). As they are pushed into the icing, the balls should lengthen and form balloon shapes.

6 Lift and place the icing over the cake. Smooth the top and sides and trim away any excess icing from around the base.

7 Color about 1 tablespoon of buttercream black or dark grey and place into a piping bag fitted with a number 1 piping nozzle. At the bottom of each balloon, pipe two triangles to give the impression of a bow and a wiggly string (Fig. b).

8 Using buttercream, stick a line of colored candies around the base of the cake and place a few extra candies on the top.

tip

If you don't want to pipe the strings on the balloons, you can paint them instead using black food color and a fine paintbrush.

a   b

Fearsome dragon ❶

Will any daring knight or princess dare to steal the fairy cakes this fearsome dragon is guarding? I think so! Because fairy cakes are so simple to make and decorate, this is a project that children could help with.

ingredients

1½ lb (750 g) green fondant

1½ oz (5 g) white fondant

Powdered sugar for rolling out

Black food color or black food color pen

6–7 square cookies or candies

About 12 decorated fairy cakes
   (see page 10)

equipment

Approx. 12" (30-cm) round dinner plate
   or cake board

Paintbrush

Piping nozzle (any)

Small sharp knife

techniques

Coloring fondant, page 63

Making fairy cakes, page 10

Embossing fondant, page 65

a

b

1 Begin with the dragon's body. Roll out about 1¼ lb (600 g) green fondant into a tapering sausage shape about 25" (65 cm) long (Fig. a).

2 Use dabs of water to stick the body in place around the outside edge of the plate.

3 Holding a piping nozzle at a slight angle, press it into the body to give the impression of scales (Fig. b).

tips

4 Pull a lump off the leftover green fondant and put to one side to use for the eyelids and ears later. Roll the rest into a sausage shape for the head. Squeeze the middle so that it goes in and stick the head against the thickest part of the body (Fig. a). Add scales.

5 Use the back of a knife to press a line around the front of the head for a mouth and the end of a paintbrush to press two holes for the nostrils.

6 To make the eyes, make two tiny white fondant almond shapes. Stick them onto the face with water. Make two tiny green fondant string shapes for eyebrows and stick over the eyes.

7 Make two tiny green carrot shapes for ears and stick onto the head. Press a paintbrush handle into each one to give a bit of definition.

8 Paint two black dots on the eyes with black food color and a paintbrush or with a black food color pen.

9 Cut about six square cookies or candies in half diagonally and press into the dragon's back to make his spikes. Use one to make the point on his tail.

10 Fill the center of the plate with decorated fairy cakes.

variation

This dinosaur is made in exactly the same way as the dragon except that once the icing had been rolled into a head shape, the back of the head was pulled and pinched to form a frill shape and it doesn't have any spikes.

a

b

Frosted flowers ❶

A design so simple, there's virtually no decorating involved! You can frost other flowers such as freesias, pansies, petunias, primulas and violets. If you choose flowers other than these, you must make sure that they are not poisonous. With deep red roses and a red or dark green ribbon, this would also make a stunning Christmas cake.

ingredients

8" (20-cm) round sponge cake (see page 10)
1 quantity buttercream (see page 26)
Powdered sugar, for rolling out
2 lb (1 kg) white or ivory fondant
1 egg white or 5 tbsp sugar dissolved in 1 tbsp hot, boiled water
½ cup (125 g) sugar

equipment

Carving knife
Palette knife
10" (25-cm) round cake board
Rolling pin
Fondant smoother (optional)
Small sharp knife
Soft paintbrush
6–8 rose blooms (washed, dried and stems cut off)
Saucer
10–12 rose leaves (washed and dried)
28" (70 cm) pink ribbon, 1½" (4 cm) wide
Adhesive tape

techniques

Filling and covering a cake with buttercream, page 27
Covering a cake with fondant, page 61
Covering a cake board, page 62
Using ribbon, page 24

1 Level the top of the cake and turn it upside down so that the flat base now forms the top of the cake. Slice the cake horizontally into two or three layers, fill the layers with buttercream and reassemble.

2 Place the cake on the cake board and spread a thin covering of buttercream around the top and sides. Place to one side.

3 Dust your work surface with powdered sugar and knead the fondant until pliable. Roll it out and lift and place over the cake. Smooth the top and sides and trim away the excess from around the base.

4 Pick out any crumbs from the leftover icing and use it to cover the cake board using the bandage method (see page 62).

5 Using a soft paintbrush, dab egg white or sugar solution around the tips of one of the rose blooms (Fig. a).

6 Dip the rose into a saucer of sugar. Shake off the excess and leave to dry (Fig. b).

7 When dry, arrange the roses and leaves on top of the cake. Place the ribbon around the base of the cake. Cut to size and use a small piece of adhesive tape to secure it at the back.

variation

This version uses silk flowers, so it's ideal for that last minute cake panic.

Scary Halloween cake ❶

Marbling is an easy effect to achieve and the ghoulish, red-veined eyeballs are also simple to make. You should be able to find jelly snake candies easily, but if you can't, roll balls of fondant into snakes instead.

ingredients

6" (15-cm) round sponge cake (see
    page 10)
1 quantity buttercream (see page 26)
1 lb 2 oz (500 g) white fondant
Powdered sugar, for rolling out
1 oz (30 g) black fondant
Red food color paste
7–8 jelly snakes
Black food color paste or black food
    color pen

equipment

Carving knife
Palette knife
10" (25-cm) round cake board
Rolling pin
Fondant smoother (optional)
Small sharp knife
Fine and medium paintbrushes

techniques

Filling and covering a cake with
    buttercream, page 27
Marbling fondant, page 64
Covering a cake with fondant, page 61
Painting on fondant, page 64

1 Level the top of the cake and turn it upside down. Slice it two or three times horizontally and sandwich the layers together with buttercream. Place the cake on the board and spread buttercream around the sides and top.

2 Pull off a 3 oz (90 g) lump of white fondant and place to one side. Dust your work surface with powdered sugar and knead the remaining white icing until soft.

3 Tear ¾ oz (20 g) of the black fondant into bits and press into the white. Roll the two colors into a thick sausage shape. Fold the sausage in half and reroll. Repeat another two or three times, then roll out (Fig. a).

4 Lift and place the icing on top of the cake and smooth the top and sides. Trim away any excess from around the base.

5 Pull a little bit off the white fondant you set aside at the beginning. Put this to one side for making highlights and snake eyes later. Roll the rest into three ball shapes for the eyeballs.

6 Divide the leftover black fondant into three and roll into three balls. Flatten the balls into discs and stick one onto each eye with a dab of water.

7 Make three tiny flat white discs and stick one onto each eye for highlights.

8 Paint blood vessels onto the eyes using red food color and a fine paintbrush (Fig. b). Stick the eyeballs in place on top of the cake with dabs of water.

9 Arrange the snakes around the top of the cake and the board. If they won't stay in place, stick them with little dabs of water.

10 Make two tiny white fondant balls for eyes for each snake and stick on with water. Using either a black food color pen or black food color and a fine paintbrush, add tiny black food color dots for pupils.

tip

For a really ghoulish surprise, you could color the cake mixture green before baking and fill with orange or purple colored buttercream.

a   b

Hearts and ribbons ❷

A stylish idea for Valentine's day or an anniversary. Ribbon insertion is a traditional form of cake decorating. Here, wide ribbon gives the cake a more contemporary feel. A variation of this cake is shown on page 61.

ingredients

7" (18-cm) square sponge cake (see page 10)
1 quantity buttercream (see page 26)
Powdered sugar, for rolling out
1½ lb (750 g) white fondant
6½ oz (200 g) red fondant
2 tbsp white royal icing (optional; see tip opposite)

equipment

Wax paper or tracing paper
Pencil
Scissors
Carving knife
Palette knife
10" (25-cm) round cake board
Rolling pin
Fondant smoother (optional)
Small sharp knife
Heart-shaped cutter
Piping bag
No. 3 piping nozzle (optional; see tip opposite)
Scalpel or small, sharp knife
1 yd (1 m) ribbon
Paintbrush

techniques

Filling and covering a cake with buttercream, page 27
Covering a cake with fondant, page 61
Embossing a pattern, page 65
Covering a board with fondant, page 62
Piping, page 98

1 Trace the heart template on page 67. Cut out. Place the template on the cake and cut around it (see Fig. b on page 39).

2 Split the cake into two or three layers and reassemble, sandwiching the layers together with buttercream. Place cake on board. Spread a thin coating of buttercream over the sides and top of the cake.

3 Dust your work surface with powdered sugar and roll out the white fondant to a thickness of about ½" (1 cm). Lift and place onto the cake and smooth the icing into position. Trim away the excess from around the base.

4 Gently press a heart-shaped cutter into the icing to leave an impression of the shape (Fig. a). Try not to go right through the icing or there's a chance the buttercream might ooze out. Repeat all over the cake.

5 Moisten the exposed cake board with a little water. Thinly roll out the red fondant. Cut it into strips and lay it around the base of the cake so that it covers the board. Trim and neaten the edges (Fig. b).

6 Place about 1 tablespoon of white royal icing into a piping bag fitted with a number 3 piping nozzle and pipe a "snail trail" (see page 98) around the base of the cake.

7 Using a scalpel or an extremely sharp knife, cut two slits the same length as the width of your ribbon about 1" (2.5 cm) apart on the side of the cake.

8 Cut about 2" (5 cm) of ribbon. Insert the ends into the slits (Fig. c). Use the scalpel to poke the ribbon in securely. Repeat two or three times over the cake.

9 Make a bow with the remaining ribbon and stick on top of the cake using either a dab of royal icing or a moistened ball of white fondant.

10 Brush away any dusty fingerprints from the board with a soft damp paintbrush.

tips

Don't want to pipe around the base of the cake? Stick small white fondant balls around it instead.

Because of the amount of fabric on this design it is not advisable to use candles.

a

b

c

Christmas gift ❷

The technique shown here is a simple form of marquetry. Icing shapes are cut out and replaced with others of an identical shape but in a different color. Despite being a Christmas design, it is not obligatory to use fruitcake. Substitute sponge cake and buttercream and omit the marzipan if you prefer.

ingredients

6" (15-cm) square fruit cake (see page 14)
3 tbsp brandy (optional)
3 tbsp boiled apricot jam
Powdered sugar, for rolling out
1 lb 2 oz (500 g) marzipan
1 lb 2 oz (500 g) white fondant
8 oz (250 g) green fondant
½ oz (45 g) red fondant

equipment

Carving knife
8" (20-cm) square cake board
Cocktail stick
Pastry brush
Rolling pin
Fondant smoother (optional)
Small sharp knife
Holly leaf cutter
1 yd (1 m) ribbon
Scissors

techniques

Covering a fruit cake with marzipan, page 85
Covering a cake with fondant, page 61

1 Level the top of the cake and turn it upside down on the cake board. Pierce the top of the cake a few times with the cocktail stick and drizzle the brandy over the top. Brush the apricot jam over the top and sides of the cake.

2 Dust your work surface with powdered sugar. Knead and roll out the marzipan. Lay the marzipan over the top of the cake and smooth the top and sides. Trim any excess from around the base.

3 Place a few light dabs of water on the surface of the marzipan. These are just to hold the fondant covering in place. If you soak the marzipan you will not be able to remove the fondant cutouts, so use a light hand.

4 Sprinkle more powdered sugar on your work surface and knead and roll out the white fondant. Lift and place over the cake. Smooth the top and sides and neaten around the base as before.

5 Press the holly leaf cutter into the cake. Try to just cut through the fondant and not the marzipan or the cake. Remove the leaf shape (Fig. a). Cut out leaf shapes all over the cake.

6 Roll out the green fondant. Try to make it roughly the same thickness as the white fondant cake covering.

7 Using the holly leaf cutter, cut out enough green leaves to replace the white ones you have cut out of the cake. Reroll the leftover green fondant as necessary.

8 Place the leaves into the gaps on the cake using dabs of water (Fig. b). Using the back of a knife, press a few lines into each leaf for veins.

9 Make tiny red fondant balls for berries. Squash them and stick onto the cake with water.

10 To tie the ribbon, pass both ends under the cake board and tie in a knot. Bring the ends back up and tie into a bow. Trim the ends if necessary to neaten them.

tips

By using different cutters, you could easily adapt this design to suit any occasion. For example, use a flower cutter and pink fondant to make a pretty birthday gift.

You could make a rectangular fondant label and pipe a message on it.

a

b

Happy gardener ③

Brown sugar makes incredibly realistic looking soil. However, it is very crunchy. For a softer alternative, dab chocolate buttercream around the top and base of the cake instead.

ingredients

8" (20-cm) square sponge cake (see page 10)
1 quantity buttercream (see page 26)
Powdered sugar for rolling out
1 lb 12 oz (800 g) cream colored fondant
2½ oz (75 g) brown fondant
Black food color
11 oz (300 g) green fondant
1 strand uncooked spaghetti
4 oz (100 g) terracotta-colored fondant (use "paprika" food color paste or a mixture of pink, yellow and white fondant)
Silver food color (optional; see tip)
½ cup (45 g) brown sugar

equipment

Carving knife
Palette knife
10" (25-cm) square cake board
Rolling pin
Fondant smoother (optional)
Small, sharp knife
Paintbrush
Piping nozzle (any)

1 Level the top of the cake and turn it over so that the base now forms the top. Slice the cake horizontally into two or three layers and then sandwich the layers back together with buttercream. Place the cake onto the board and thinly coat the sides and top of the cake with buttercream.

2 Dust your work surface with powdered sugar. Knead the cream colored fondant until pliable and roll it out to a thickness of about ⅜" (1 cm). Lift and place over the cake. Smooth the top and sides and trim away the excess with a sharp knife.

3 To make the gardener, roll 2 oz (60 g) brown fondant into a sausage shape, 7" (18 cm) long. Bend it into a horseshoe shape (Fig. a). Slice the ends off and stick in the center of the cake with a dab of water.

4 Knead a little black food color into about 5 oz (150 g) of green fondant to make a khaki color. Roll about 3 oz (90 g) into a conical shape for his body. Flatten the base and top slightly and stick on top of the legs with a little water.

5 To keep the man upright, stick a strand of spaghetti into the body. Leave a bit protruding for the head.

6 Roll about 1 oz (30 g) terracotta fondant into a ball for the man's head. Stick it on top of the body (Fig. b). Poke the edge of a piping nozzle into the lower part of the face to make a smile.

7 Make three tiny terracotta ball shapes. Use these for the ears and nose and stick them in position. Poke a hollow into each ear with the end of a paintbrush.

8 Roll ⅓ oz (10 g) khaki green fondant into a ball and flatten it to make the cap. Stick on top of his head and press a line into the front of the cap with the back of a knife.

9 Roll about ¾ oz (20 g) khaki green fondant into a sausage. Cut it in half to make his arms. Stick one either side of his body.

10 For boots, make two ½ oz (15 g) khaki green sausages. Bend into "L" shapes and stick onto the legs. Press four lines into the sole of each boot with the back of a knife.

11 To make a flowerpot, roll ½ oz (15 g) terracotta fondant into a conical shape. Flatten the base and top. Roll and cut out a long thin terracotta strip and stick around the top of the pot (Fig. c). Make three pots and stick around the man. Paint a black food color dot on the base of each pot.

12 Make two fondant balls for the man's hands; flatten slightly. Stick one on the end of each arm, one resting on top of a flowerpot.

13 To make a spade, roll ⅓ oz (10 g) brown fondant into a long string. Cut a small section off the end and lay across the top of the longer section to form a "T" shape. Stick onto the cake and add a square cream piece for the blade.

a   b   c

14 For the trowel, roll a tiny bit of brown fondant into a pellet shape for the handle. Make a similar cream shape for the blade. Press a paintbrush handle into the blade to give it a curved shape. Stick onto the cake.

15 Paint the relevant bits of the trowel and spade silver, with food color.

16 Use the remaining green fondant to make the leaves. Roll it out thinly and cut out simple leaf shapes. Press a couple of veins into each leaf with the back of a knife, put a dab of water onto the back of each leaf and stick them around the sides of the cake.

17 To finish, moisten the top of the cake with a little water and carefully spoon the sugar around the character. Do the same around the leaves on the cake board.

tip

If you cannot get silver food color, use grey fondant to make the trowel and spade blades instead.

Christening cake ③

At first glance, this may look like a terribly complicated cake to attempt but it isn't as tricky as it looks. You can take your time over it. The top plaque with the bootees can be made weeks in advance. This pretty broderie anglaise technique works just as well in blue (see Baby's cradle on page 108).

ingredients

8" (20-cm) square sponge cake (see page 10)

1 quantity buttercream (see page 26)

Powdered sugar, for rolling out

2 lb 4 oz (1 kg) white fondant

1 lb 2 oz (500 g) pink fondant

1 quantity royal icing (see page 90)

Pink food color

equipment

Carving knife

Palette knife

12" (30-cm) square cake board

Rolling pin

Fondant smoother (optional)

Small, sharp knife

Paintbrush

3 piping bags (see page 96)

No. 1 and star piping nozzles

Wax paper or tracing paper

Pencil

Scissors

1 yd (1 m) thin, pink ribbon

techniques

Filling and covering a cake with buttercream, page 27

Covering a cake with fondant, page 61

Covering a cake board with fondant, page 62

Piping, page 98

1 To prepare the cake, level the top and turn it upside down. Slice it horizontally into two or three layers, fill with buttercream and reassemble. Place it in the center of the cake board and spread buttercream around the sides and top.

2 Dust your work surface with powdered sugar and knead and roll out 1 lb 10 oz (800 g) white fondant. Lift and place over the cake. Smooth the top and sides and trim and neaten around the base.

a   b   c

3 Lightly moisten the visible cake board and thinly roll out about 12 oz (350 g) pink fondant. Cut into four strips and use it to cover the cake board (see page 62). Trim and neaten the edges.

4 Using a paintbrush handle, press a series of dots and dashes into the pink icing to form a pattern. The center of a flower is a dot and a series of six dashes around the outside form the petals (refer to Fig. a). Place about 3 tablespoons of white royal icing into a piping bag fitted with a star nozzle and pipe a "snail trail" around the base of the cake.

5 To make the plaque, roll out another 5 oz (150 g) pink fondant. Trace the template on page 67 and cut out. Place the template onto the pink fondant and cut out the flower shape. Using the paintbrush, press a line of dots around the outside of the shape and a circle of dot and dash flowers just inside (Fig. a).

6 Place about 1 tablespoon of white royal icing into a piping bag fitted with a number 1 piping nozzle. Carefully pipe around the outside of all the dots and dashes on both the board and the plaque (Fig. b).

7 Place a few dabs of water on top of the cake. Using a palette knife, carefully lift and place the plaque into position.

8 To make the bootees, make two ½ oz (15 g) white fondant balls. Squash both into flattish oval shapes. Take another two ½ oz (15 g) lumps of white and roll out. Cut out two rectangles about 5" (12 cm) long. Round the corners of the rectangles slightly.

9 Fold a rectangle around the top of an oval to form a bootee (Fig. c). Poke a few lace holes with the end of a paintbrush. Repeat with the second bootee, then stick them in place on the plaque with a light dab of water.

10 Color about 2 tablespoons of royal icing pink and place in a piping bag with a number 1 piping nozzle. Pipe a couple of lines on each bootee to make the laces.

11 Pipe a zigzag pattern around the edges of the plaque to hide any rough edges.

12 Pipe a small floral pattern on each of the four corners of the cake using a series of dots and dashes.

13 Make four tiny pink ribbon bows and stick in position with royal icing dots.

tip

When using a fine piping nozzle, it helps if you make the icing slightly runnier than usual by stirring in a few drops of water.

variation

A plaque this shape suits all sorts of other shaped cakes as well. Here the plaque has been decorated more intricately. You could pipe the baby's name in the center if you wish.

MARZIPAN

Made out of ground almonds, the difference between marzipan and almond paste is that marzipan contains a higher proportion of almonds so is usually a little more expensive. The taste is very similar and they behave the same way when working with them. You can make your own marzipan or you can buy it. It is readily available from shops in two shades; the traditional yellow (labelled "gold") or white. It can be colored using food color so could be used instead of fondant on most of the designs on pages 68–83.

Recipe

This recipe lightly cooks the eggs and produces a marzipan that is fairly firm and not too oily. (If you are concerned about the eggs being only lightly cooked, see page 4, use ready-made marzipan instead.)

ingredients

(Amounts for 1 lb (500 g))

1 whole egg and one egg yolk

½ cup (110 g) sugar

1 cup (110 g) powdered sugar (sifted)

1⅓ cups (225 g) ground almonds

A few drops of almond extract

1 Put the eggs and sugars into a heatproof bowl and place over a pan of hot water. Whisk until thick and creamy.

2 Remove the bowl from the heat and add a few drops of almond extract. Using a wooden spoon, stir in the ground almonds, then lightly knead into a ball. The marzipan will firm up slightly as it cools, but if you feel it is still too soft, add a little more powdered sugar.

STORING: Ideally this should be used as soon as possible but if you have to store it for a day or so, double-wrap it in a small plastic bag or plastic wrap and keep in the refrigerator. Use within a week.

TIP If the marzipan is hard to knead, microwave it for 10–15 seconds. Test it and repeat if necessary. Don't overdo it as the oils in the center can burn.

ABOVE *Marzipan shapes are quick and easy to make.*

QUANTITY GUIDE

Although amounts will vary depending upon how thick you like your marzipan, here is a rough guide to the quantities you require to cover different sized cakes.

Round cake	6" (15cm)	7" (18cm)	8" (20cm)	9" (23cm)	10" (25cm)	11" (28cm)	12" (30cm)	
Square cake		6" (15cm)	7" (18cm)	8" (20cm)	9" (23cm)	10" (25cm)	11" (28cm)	12" (30cm)
Marzipan	1lb (500g)	1lb 5oz (650g)	1lb 10oz (800g)	2lb (900g)	2lb 8oz (1.1kg)	3lb (1.4kg)	3lb 8oz (1.6kg)	4lb (1.8kg)

Covering a fruit cake for fondant or swirled royal icing

Because razor sharp edges are not required for fondant or swirled royal icing, the whole cake can be covered in one step.

1 Place the cake in position on the board. If the top is slightly domed, slice this off and place the cake upside down on the board. Plug any holes left by currants with small balls of marzipan. If you want to, drizzle a little brandy over the top of the cake and allow it to sink in. Heat some apricot jam in a small saucepan or in a bowl in the microwave to boiling point and brush over the top and sides of the cake. Knead the marzipan. Dust your work surface with powdered sugar and roll it out (Fig. a).

2 Carefully lift the marzipan and place it on the cake (Fig. b).

3 Ease it over the top and sides of the cake and gently press into position. Trim away the excess from around the base (Fig. c).

4 Smooth over the top and sides with the flat of your hands. Ideally then use a fondant smoother (Fig. d).

a

b

c

d

Covering a round fruit cake for smooth royal icing

1 If the top of the cake is rounded, level it so that it is flat and turn the cake over. Fill any holes with small balls of marzipan. Drizzle a little brandy over the cake if you wish and allow it to sink in. Heat some apricot jam in a small saucepan or in a bowl in the microwave to boiling point and brush over the top of the cake (Fig. a).

2 Knead about two thirds of the marzipan and roll it out to no less than ¼" (5 mm) thickness. Place the cake upside down on the marzipan and cut around the edge (Fig. b).

3 Turn the cake the right way up and place on the board. Measure the circumference of the cake and make a note of the measurement. Spread jam around the sides. Knead and roll out the rest of the marzipan (including the trimmings). Cut a strip the same length as the circumference of the cake and as wide as the height of the cake, including the marzipan topping (Fig. c).

4 Roll the marzipan strip up like a bandage and unwind it around the sides of the cake (Fig. d).

5 Leave to dry for at least 48 hours before icing. It is important that the surfaces, edges and corners of the marzipan are smooth and sharp, as any crinkle or bump will show through the royal icing.

Covering a square fruit cake for smooth royal icing

1 Level the top of the cake if necessary and brush it with boiled apricot jam (Fig. a).

2 Knead about two thirds of the marzipan and roll it out to no less than ¼" (5 mm) thickness. Place the cake, upside down on the marzipan. Trim around the cake (Fig. b) and place it right side up on the board.

3 Measure the length and width of one side of the cake. Cut four strips of marzipan using those measurements (Fig. c).

4 Spread jam over the sides and stick the strips of marzipan onto the cake (Fig. d).

5 Leave the cake to dry for at least 48 hours before icing. Make sure that all of the surfaces, edges and corners are as smooth and sharp as possible.

a

b

c

d

Coloring marzipan

It is easy to color marzipan. Simply add color (paste or gel colors work best as they're less likely to make the marzipan soggy) and knead in. Because gold marzipan is already quite a strong color, it will distort some colors such as blue and give them a greenish tint. Therefore, if you're planning to color marzipan, it's best to use the white variety.

1 Apply the color to the marzipan with a cocktail stick (Fig. a).

2 Knead the color into the marzipan, ensuring that it is

evenly blended (Fig. b).

Modelling with marzipan

The principles of modelling with marzipan are the same as those for fondant (see pages 66). You can make models of virtually anything – people, animals, flowers etc. Use water to stick the pieces of marzipan together.

Little fruits like these are fun and easy to make. They

could be used as cake decorations or even as sweet treats at Christmas. The blush on the apple was made by brushing a little edible dusting powder over the green. You could achieve a similar effect by dabbing a little red food color on the apple instead.

ABOVE *On this design, nuts were arranged on top of the fruit cake before baking and glazed with boiled apricot jam when the cake had cooled. A pattern of simple marzipan Santas stand around the edges. You could use stars if you prefer.*

RIGHT *Marzipan fruits are a very simple way to create a beautifully decorated cake. The edge is simply crimped (see page 65) and the cake and board trimmed with a yellow ribbon.*

ROYAL ICING

Royal icing is extremely versatile. Made from egg whites and powdered sugar, it can be used for both covering and piping cakes. It has a more crisp texture than fondant and gives a cake a very classic, polished look. It sets hard, so can be used to create all sorts of extravagant effects. When using royal icing it is important that all of your bowls and utensils are dry and grease-free, so give them a wash in hot soapy water before you start. It may take a few attempts to perfect your technique with royal icing, but the finished result is worth the effort.

Recipe

If you are using royal icing to coat a cake, it is essential that you include glycerine and lemon juice. The glycerine enables you to get a knife cleanly through the icing when you cut the cake and the lemon juice keeps the icing white.

If you are just making icing to pipe flowers, snail trail around a cake or to make the runouts on the Snowflakes (see pages 112–113) and Baby's cradle (see pages 108–109) cakes, you can leave these two items out.

There is a slight risk of salmonella from using raw egg (see note page 4). If you prefer, you can used dried egg white substitute; refer to the instructions on the packet.

ingredients
(Amounts for 1 quantity)

2 egg whites (or equivalent amount of dried egg white, reconstituted)

3½ cups (450 g) powdered sugar, sifted

1 tsp (5 ml) lemon juice

1 tsp (5 ml) glycerine

1 Reconstitute the egg white following the instructions on the packet. This normally means adding a couple of teaspoons of water and mixing it to a smooth paste. Add the rest of the water gradually, beating well until light and frothy.

2 Stir in about a quarter of the powdered sugar. If using a food mixer, set it to the slowest speed.

3 Gradually add the rest of the sugar, the lemon juice and glycerine.

4 Beat until the icing stands up in peaks. If you're using a food mixer, beat on slow speed for 5 minutes. Don't be tempted to race ahead on a fast speed or your icing will be too full of air bubbles to use properly.

STORING: When the icing is ready, transfer to a clean, grease-free plastic food container with a tight fitting lid. Lay a sheet of plastic wrap directly on top of the icing to prevent it drying out and place the lid back on the container. Always keep the icing covered when not in use and use within a week.

USING: If you have stored the icing, you need to remix it before using. Take a few tablespoons of icing out of the container and place in a small bowl. Beat it thoroughly with a knife to get rid of air bubbles and to make it nice and smooth. If you want to keep the leftover beaten icing from hardening, place a damp cloth over the top of the bowl.

Quantity guide
It is difficult to give even a rough guide for this as it really depends on how thick you want your covering of icing to be. If you have a lot of cakes to cover it is best to make up double the amount shown in the recipe and use that up before making another batch.

Coloring royal icing

It is possible to use either liquid or paste colors. If using liquid color, don't add too much as you could overthin the icing and make it too runny to hold its shape when piping. If you are trying to achieve a pale color, note that the icing will darken slightly as it dries.

1 Add the color sparingly to the icing (Fig. a).

2 Mix until the icing is evenly colored (Fig. b). If you want to keep excess icing useable in case you need more, lay a damp cloth over the top of the bowl.

Peaked and swirled effects

These are the easiest finishes to achieve on a royal iced cake as you don't have to be precise at all.

To get peaks in the icing, simply spread royal icing over the cake, press the palette knife into the icing and pull away sharply to leave a peak (Fig. c).

A swirly effect is achieved by simply swirling the icing about the cake as you cover it (Fig. d). This effect was used on Christmas bows (above and pages 102–103).

Royal-icing a square fruit cake

This technique is only used on a fruit cake which has been covered with marzipan, never on sponge. You will need a "straightedge" which is like a metal ruler but has no markings on it and also a cake scraper to produce a smooth finish. It will take about a week to coat the cake because the icing has to dry between layers.

1 Spread some icing over the top of the cake with a palette knife. Spread it back and forth a few times to get rid of any air bubbles, then spread it over the whole of the top of the cake. Cover the surface as evenly as possible (Fig. a).

2 Remove the excess icing from around the edges (Fig. b).

3 Take the straightedge and place it at the far end of the cake. Pull it towards you in one continuous movement (Fig. c). You should be left with a thin covering over the cake.

4 Remove the excess icing from around the edges (Fig. d) and leave the cake to dry for a minimum of three hours, preferably overnight.

5 Spread icing over one side of the cake (Fig. e).

6 Remove the excess icing from the top edge and the corners (Fig. f).

7 Stand the cake scraper at the far end of the cake and pull it toward you in one movement (Fig. g).

8 Remove the excess icing from the top edge and corners again (Fig. h). Leave to dry for another couple of hours.

9 Cover the other sides in the same way, then leave the cake to dry overnight (Fig. i).

10 Ice the cake with another two layers allowing drying time between coats.

Covering a square cake board

Make sure that the royal iced cake is completely dry before putting it on a board, otherwise you may damage its finish.

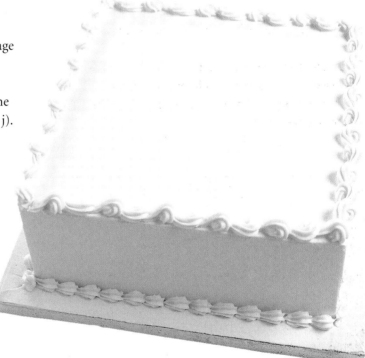

1 Spread a thin layer of royal icing over one side of the board. Remove the excess icing from the edge (Fig. j).

2 Pull the cake scraper over the icing toward you in one movement (Fig. k).

3 Remove the excess from the edges (Fig. l) and repeat on the opposite side. Leave to dry for at least 3 hours and cover the other two sides. Repeat with a second layer for a neat finish.

Royal-icing a round fruit cake

As well as a straightedge and cake scraper, you will need an icing turntable. This technique is only used on a fruit cake which has been covered with marzipan, never on sponge. You need to allow a week to do this, as the icing has to dry between layers.

1 Cover the top surface of the cake in the same way as described for the square cake (see page 92) and leave to dry overnight (Fig. a).

2 Spread royal icing around the sides of the cake (Fig. b).

3 Remove the excess icing from around the top edge with a palette knife (Fig. c).

4 Place the cake on the turntable. Hold the cake scraper vertically at the back of the cake; hold the board and turntable with your other hand. Turn the turntable in one revolution, pulling the scraper toward you (Fig. d). Lift the scraper off the cake (this will leave a mark).

5 Neaten the top edge again (Fig. e). Leave the cake to dry overnight. Repeat the process, building up at least three layers.

Covering a round cake board

1 Stand the cake on a turntable. Spread a thin, even layer of royal icing around the board (Fig. f).

2 Remove the excess from the edges using a palette knife (Fig. g).

3 Run the cake scraper around the cake board in one continuous fluid motion (Fig. h).

4 Remove the excess from the edges again (Fig. i) and leave to dry for at least 3 hours. Repeat with a second coat.

Piping

The thought of piping can be a bit terrifying. However, if you have the right equipment and a bit of time to practice, anyone can learn some simple techniques.

There are a number of different piping sets available, from shiny syringe-type contraptions to the humble bit of folded wax paper. It is even possible to buy tubes of ready-made piping icing from the supermarket that come with a set of different nozzles that you screw onto the end. There is no right or wrong piece of equipment, use whatever suits you.

Piping bags

WASHABLE POLYESTER PIPING BAGS These have certain advantages. Obviously, because they're washable they're reusable. They don't split and burst at inopportune moments and grease from buttercream doesn't seep through the sides. They are used with a connector to which you attach the piping nozzle. This means you can change the piping nozzle without having to set up a new bag. They're also handy for making meringues.

DISPOSABLE STORE-BOUGHT BAGS These are very convenient as they're already made up for you. There's no need to wash them after you've finished icing, you can just throw them away. Their only disadvantage is their expense.

HOMEMADE WAX PAPER PIPING BAGS Definitely the cheapest option, as you can make hundreds of piping bags from one roll of wax paper. They are quite easy to make; see the instructions opposite.

BELOW *Piping equipment can be as simple and cheap as a homemade piping bag or as easy as store-bought tubes of ready-made icing.*

ABOVE *This pretty cradle is made entirely out of piped royal icing (see pages 108–109).*

Making a piping bag

1 Cut some wax paper into a triangle.

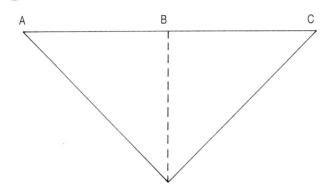

2 Pick up corner "C" and fold over, so that "B" forms a sharp cone in the center.

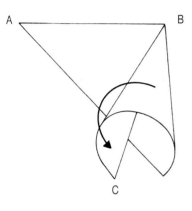

3 Wrap corner "A" around the cone.

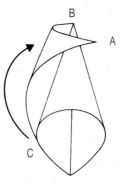

4 Make sure that "A" and "C" are at the back and that the point of the cone is sharp.

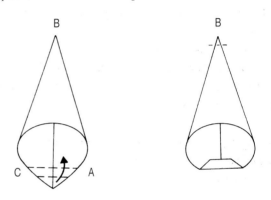

5 Fold points "A" and "C" inside the top edge of the bag to hold it securely. Snip off the end "B" and insert a nozzle.

Filling a piping bag

Usually you pipe with a piping nozzle in the end of the bag. If using a disposable or wax paper bag, snip about ½" (12 mm) off the end of the bag and drop a piping nozzle inside.

1 Scoop up some icing on a palette knife and place it inside the bag. Holding the knife through the bag, pull the knife out (Fig. a).

2 To close the bag, fold the end over a couple of times and force the icing down into the nozzle (Fig. b).

Different piping effects

There are many different types of piping nozzle available that enable you to create all sorts of wondrous patterns and effects. Many are made in plastic as well as metal. The difference (apart from the price) being that metal nozzles have slightly more accurate edges and create a sharper effect, and they also tend to last a bit longer.

Piping is just a question of pressure. You squeeze the bag and the icing comes out. Release the pressure and it stops. It really is that simple. That's not to say that you won't have the odd mishap here and there, but most are easy to correct or disguise and after a very short time you'll be amazed at what you can do.

Here are a few of the most common nozzles and the effects you can achieve with them (Fig. a from top to bottom).

NUMBER 2 This has a simple round hole at its tip. It's ideal for piping thin lines, writing, piping dots and tiny "snail trails" around the edges of things. It is also easy to use a nozzle like this to make a simple floral pattern, composed of dots and dashes.

NUMBER 4 This has a bigger hole in the end than the number 2, so can be used for more dramatic effects. You can pipe dots, dashes and even big flowers such as the ones on the Summer flowers cake on page 48.

STAR As its name suggests, the serrated edges of this nozzle are ideal for piping star shapes. You can pipe single stars or even cover a whole cake (see Buttercream flowers on page 42). You can also use a nozzle like this to pipe a line of shells around the edges or base of a cake. See the instructions for "snail trail" opposite.

PETAL Shaped a bit like a teardrop, this nozzle is ideal for piping flowers.

LEAF A very useful nozzle. It enables you to pipe leaf shapes quickly and easily. Wiggle the bag slightly as you pull it away and you end up with a lovely serrated effect.

SNAIL TRAIL (See the first three examples in Fig. a.) This is a common technique used for piping around the base or edges of cakes. Using a nozzle with a plain or star-shaped tip, you squeeze a little icing out of the nozzle, release the pressure and pull along slightly so the icing tapers into a slight point. Keeping the nozzle still in the icing, squeeze another blob out and repeat.

Piping without a nozzle

You can pipe with a bag alone. However, the bag must be used right away before the end becomes soggy and distorted or the icing sets and blocks it. Fill and close the bag before cutting anything off the end. (Fig. b from top to bottom.)

SNIP STRAIGHT ACROSS THE END OF THE BAG, REMOVING A TINY TRIANGLE Use this bag as you would a number 2 piping nozzle. The larger the triangle you cut off the end, the thicker the line the bag will produce.

SNIP THE END OF THE BAG INTO A POINT You can make leaf shapes. Squeeze a little icing out of the end and release the pressure. Pull the bag away so that the icing tapers away into a tail.

SNIP A "V" SHAPE INTO THE END OF THE BAG This produces piping that has an interesting ridge along its back.

Multicolored piping

On page 28 there is a demonstration, using buttercream, of how you can place more than one color in a piping bag at a time. It is possible to do this with royal icing too.

Piped flowers

Piping a simple five-petal blossom is a worthwhile technique to try to master as it means that as well as blossoms, you can also pipe violets and primroses. To make violets, color the icing purple and for primroses, color it yellow (see page 91).

You will need an icing nail (which looks like a big woodwork nail) or mini turntable which you can revolve in your fingers. Alternatively, you could use a piece of cork stuck on the end of a long nail instead.

1 Place the petal nozzle into a piping bag with about two tablespoons of colored icing. Fold the end of the bag over to close it.

2 Stick a square of wax paper onto the top of the piping nail with a dab of icing.

3 With the thick end of the piping nozzle in the center of the flower, squeeze the bag and turn the nail. Slightly lift the thin edge of the nozzle as you turn, to form a petal. Release the pressure and pull away.

4 Wipe the end of the nozzle. Tuck the nozzle just underneath the edge of the first petal and pipe a second. Repeat, making five petals in total (Fig. c). Remove from the nail or turntable and leave to dry on the paper. Add a yellow dot in the center to finish (Fig. d, top).

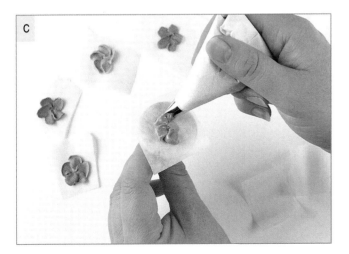

DAISY Pipe white lines fanning out in a circle and pipe a dot of yellow in the center (Fig. d, center).

HYACINTH Pipe a central green stem then, using a star nozzle, pipe a few stars either side (Fig. d, bottom).

Piping lettering

There are various ways to position and pipe your message on top of a cake. This technique does require practice, as you have to get used to writing with icing instead of a pen. You will develop your own style of "piping writing" and know instinctively how much space you will need for your message.

SCRIBING A relatively simple way to transfer your message onto a cake covered in fondant or royal icing is by scribing. The cake should have been left to stand overnight so the surface has hardened.

Write your message on a piece of wax paper and place it into position on the cake. Using a scribing tool (a bit like a paintbrush handle with a sharp point on the end) or a dressmaker's pin, trace over the lettering. When you remove the wax paper, you should be able to see your message faintly scratched on the cake's surface. Use this as a guide to pipe over.

FREEHAND This is what you are ultimately aiming for: to be able to write freehand on your cakes. However, even professionals have difficulty sometimes. Beware the word "Congratulations". It's quite long and always seems to take up more room than you think!

Using a letterpress

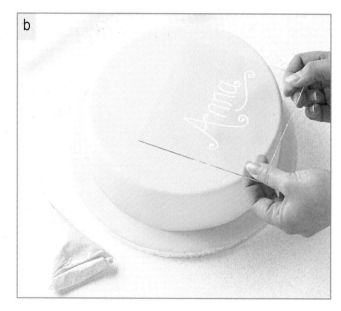

Usually used on fondant or buttercream cakes where they can leave a mark, these ingenious gadgets allow you to build your message on a plaque which you then press into the icing. An imprint is left behind for you to pipe over. There are various styles available which can be bought from cake decorating shops, alternatively you can make your own.

1 Write your message in pencil on a piece of wax paper. Turn the paper over so the message is backward and place a small piece of acrylic on top. Place a number 2 piping nozzle in a piping bag and pipe over the words with royal icing (Fig. a). Leave the lettering to dry.

2 Cover the cake with fondant or buttercream. Turn the acrylic over and press into the cake to leave an imprint behind (Fig. b). Use this as a guide to pipe over.

Piped decorations

There are many types of piped royal icing decorations that you can make. Small models, such as the cradle on page 108, are made in sections then stuck together with royal icing. You can pipe onto fondant plaques too. One of their main advantages is that they can be made well in advance. Store the finished decorations in a box away from dust and daylight.

Runouts

This technique of piping an outline then flooding it with watered down royal icing is explained in full in the Baby's cradle and Snowflakes cakes on pages 108 and 112.

However, as well as making shapes, runouts can also be used to make lettering (Fig. c). When dry, gently ease the letters off the waxed paper with a palette knife and fix in place with a dab of royal icing.

Templates

Baby's cradle (pages 108–109)

Head—make one

Rockers—make four

Canopy—make one of each

Foot—make one

Sides—make two

Base—make one

Wedding star (pages 104–105)

Snowflakes (pages 112–113)

All of the templates are shown at 100%.

royal icing

Christmas bows ❶

This simple idea makes a stunning Christmas centerpiece. It also works well with colored ribbon.

ingredients

7" (18-cm) round fruit cake (see page 14)
3 tbsp brandy (optional)
3 tbsp boiled apricot jam
Powdered sugar for rolling out
1¼ lb (600 g) marzipan
1 quantity white royal icing (see page 90)

equipment

Carving knife
Cocktail stick
9" (23-cm) round cake board
Pastry brush
Rolling pin
Fondant smoother (optional)
Spatula
Small, sharp knife
Palette knife
1 yd (1 m) silver and gold ribbon
Scissors

techniques

Covering a round cake with marzipan, page 86
Covering a cake with swirled royal icing, page 91

1 Level the top of the cake and turn it upside down. Pierce the top a few times with a cocktail stick and drizzle brandy over the top.

2 Place onto the cake board and brush the top and sides with boiled apricot jam.

3 Dust your work surface with powdered sugar and knead and roll out the marzipan. Lift the marzipan and place over the top of the cake. Smooth the top and sides, and trim and neaten the base.

4 Spread the royal icing over the cake and board. Swirl it into peaks using the palette knife (Fig. a). Leave the cake to dry.

5 When the icing has hardened, make four bows and stick on to the cake with dabs of royal icing.

variation

You can use any color scheme on this cake. Here, green and red give the cake a more vibrant and traditional look.

tip

As this is a fruit cake, you can make and decorate the cake at the beginning of December to avoid a panic nearer to Christmas.

a

b

Wedding star ❷

Stylish, elegant, modern—but best of all, easy to do. These instructions are based on using fruit cake and royal icing. However you could use sponge cake as a base if you prefer. Omit the marzipan and split, fill and cover the sponges with scrumptious white chocolate ganache or buttercream instead of royal icing.

ingredients

1 lb 2 oz (500 g) white fondant

Powdered sugar, for rolling out

10" (25-cm) round fruit cake

8" (20-cm) round fruit cake (alternatively, to save a bit of time, you could rent star-shaped baking pans)

5–6 tbsp brandy (optional)

4–5 tbsp boiled apricot jam

4½ lb (2.6 kg) marzipan

2 quantities white royal icing (see page 90)

equipment

13" (32-cm) petal-shaped cake board or a 12" (30-cm) round board

11" (28-cm) petal-shaped cake board or a 10" (25-cm) round board

Rolling pin

Fondant smoother (optional)

Small sharp knife

Pencil

Wax paper or tracing paper

Ruler

Scissors

Carving knife

Pastry brush

Palette knife

1 small votive candle

Small square of aluminum foil

About 16 cream rose blooms, washed, dried and stems cut off

About 20 rose leaves, washed and dried

3 yd (3 m) white ribbon, ½" (1cm) wide, for edging boards (see page 24)

Double-sided tape

2-tier chrome cake stand (see page 24)

1 Cover the cake boards using the all-in-one method (see page 62). Use 8 oz (250 g) white fondant for the larger board and 5 oz (150 g) white fondant for the smaller one. Place to one side.

2 Make templates for the cakes. Trace around the pans used for baking the cakes. Draw two identical triangles inside each circle to create a star shape (see diagram on page 101). Cut out.

3 Place the relevant template on top of each cake and cut out (Fig. a).

4 Drizzle each cake with a little brandy if you wish and coat the top with boiled apricot jam.

5 Dust your work surface with powdered sugar and roll out 1 lb 2 oz (500 g) marzipan. Run a knife underneath to check it's not stuck to the work surface and lay the largest cake upside down on the marzipan. Cut the marzipan around the cake, then turn the cake the right side up.

6 Spread boiled apricot jam around the sides. Roll out 2 lb 4 oz (1 kg) marzipan and cut out a strip about 38" (96 cm) long and the same width as the height of the cake, including the marzipan topping.

7 Roll the strip into a loose bandage and unroll around the sides of the cake (Fig b). Because the icing will have a textured finish it is not essential that all the sides are absolutely perfect, however it is important to make sure the cake is sealed in by the marzipan and there are no holes anywhere.

8 Repeat the procedure on the smaller cake using about 12 oz (350 g) marzipan for the top and 1½ lb (750 g) marzipan for the sides.

9 Carefully place the cakes into position on the covered boards (see tip opposite). If the cake is well sealed, it can be left in this state in a cake box for up to two weeks, before icing.

10 When ready, cover the cakes with royal icing. Use a palette knife to apply the icing, swirling it into peaks as you go (see Fig. a page 103). Leave a flat area in the center of the smaller cake ready for the candle.

11 Stick some double-sided tape around the edge of the boards and then secure the ribbon in place. The ends of the ribbon should meet at the back of the cake.

a   b   c

12 Add the finishing touches to the cake on the day of the wedding. Place a candle on a small piece of aluminum foil in the center of the top cake. Lay one large rose leaf over a star point and place a rose on top. Continue around the candle and add a few extra leaves if you wish (Fig. c). Repeat on the lower cake and place the cakes on to the stand.

tips

It is not advisable to use silk flowers with candles because of the possible risk of fire.

It is not essential and will not affect the taste of the cake, but if you want to prevent the fondant beneath the cake from going soggy, place the relevant star template on top of the covered board and cut around it. Remove the icing from the center of the board. When ready, sit the marzipanned cake in the hole.

Christmas stars ❷

These stencilled stars are very easy to do and are incredibly effective. Depending on your chosen color scheme, you can leave them white or accent them with silver or pale blue food color instead of gold. Instead of using traditional fruit cake covered with royal icing as a base, you could cover a marzipanned fruit cake or buttercreamed sponge cake with fondant instead.

ingredients

(See "Covering the cake" for the amount of icing required to cover cake)

7" (18-cm) round fruit or sponge cake (see pages 10–14)

1 quantity white royal icing (for making stars; see page 90)

3 tbsp brandy (optional)

3 tbsp boiled apricot jam

Powdered sugar, for rolling out

1 lb 5 oz (650 g) marzipan

Edible gold food color

Edible gold and/or silver balls

equipment

Pencil

Wax paper or baking parchment

Scalpel

Ruler

9" (23-cm) round cake board

Palette knife

Paintbrush

techniques

Filling and covering a cake with buttercream, page 27

Covering a cake with marzipan, pages 85–86/fondant, page 61/royal icing, page 94

COVERING THE CAKE

Fruit cake with marzipan and royal icing: follow the instructions on pages 86 and 94. Use about 1 lb 5 oz (650 g) marzipan and two quantities royal icing.

Fruit cake with marzipan and fondant: follow the instructions on pages 85 and 61. Use about 1 lb 5 oz (650 g) marzipan and 1 lb 2 oz (500 g) white fondant. Moisten the marzipan with water before covering it with the fondant.

Sponge cake with fondant: split and fill the cake with buttercream then spread buttercream around the outside (see page 27). Follow the instructions on page 61 for covering with fondant. Use about 1 lb 2 oz (500 g) white fondant.

1 Trace the star shapes onto the paper and cut them out using the scalpel and ruler. Make at least eight as you may only be able to use them once.

2 If not already in place, put the covered cake on the cakeboard. Place the stencil on the cake and stipple some royal icing onto the cake's surface using the flat edge of a palette knife (Fig. a).

3 Lift the stencil off the cake's surface and repeat the process over the sides and top.

4 When you have finished the stars, spread a covering of royal icing over the exposed cake board. Use the flat side of the knife to pat the icing to form little peaks. Leave the cake to dry.

5 When the royal icing has set, accent the stencil with the gold food color. Hold the brush almost flat and stroke it across the stars so that the color only coats the tips of the icing peaks (Fig. b). Do the same on the cakeboard.

6 Stick edible gold balls over the cake to fill the spaces between the stars.

tips

You may be able to find washable, reusable, plastic star-shaped stencils at a cake decorating store which will save you making your own.

You may find it helpful to use tweezers to handle the gold balls as they are tiny.

Baby's cradle ③

This pretty little cradle is made using a technique called royal icing "runouts". The outline of each crib section is piped with royal icing then flooded with slightly watered down icing. It may take a little bit of practice to get this technique right, but the results are worthwhile. One advantage to runouts is that they can be made up to a month in advance. Prepare and ice the cake in exactly the same way as the Christening cake on page 82. Use blue or pink as appropriate.

ingredients
(for the cradle only)

1 quantity white royal icing (see page 90)

½ oz (15 g) white fondant

⅛ oz (5 g) peach-colored fondant

Food color for baby's hair

½ oz (15 g) blue fondant

equipment
(for the cradle only)

Pencil

Wax paper or tracing paper

Baking parchment

Board or tray

Adhesive tape

Small cups or bowls

Palette knife

Piping bags (see page 96)

No. 1 piping nozzle

Scissors

Small, soft paintbrush

Drinking straw

Tiny ribbon bow

techniques

Runouts, page 100

Modelling with fondant, page 66

tip
Use a soft, damp paintbrush to smooth away any unwanted blobs of icing along the joins of the cradle.

1 Trace the templates of the cradle components (see page 101) onto wax paper or tracing paper.

2 Place a piece of wax paper onto something flat, such as a board or tray, and hold it in place with a small piece of tape at each corner. Slide the tracing paper underneath the wax paper. Leave an end poking out so that you can move it around freely beneath the top paper.

3 Place about a tablespoon of white royal icing into a cup and beat it thoroughly with a knife to expel any air. Stir in a couple of drops of water to help it flow through the tiny piping nozzle more easily.

4 Place the icing into a piping bag fitted with a number 1 piping nozzle. Close the bag and pipe the outlines of the cradle components.

5 Pipe at least two sides, one head end, one foot end, two canopies, four rockers and one base. It would be wise to pipe extras of each shape as the runouts will be fragile.

6 To make the icing for flooding , place two heaping tablespoons of royal icing into a bowl. Add water drop by drop. Mix until the

consistency is such that when you lift the knife out, the tail it leaves disappears on a count of three.

7 Tip or spoon the icing into a piping bag. Close the bag and snip a tiny triangle off the end. Gently squeeze the bag and using a gentle wiggling motion, fill one of the shapes. Use the tip of a soft, damp paintbrush to coax it into any obstinate corners (Fig. a). Leave to dry for at least 24 hours.

8 When dry, peel the backing off the shapes. Turn the canopy sections over and pipe crisscrossing lines on the back (Fig. b). Stick two sets of rockers together and leave these and the canopies to dry.

9 To make the pillow, make a tiny, white fondant rectangle. Using the tip of a paintbrush handle, press a line of indents down each shorter side to look like a frill (Fig. c).

10 Make a peach-colored ball for the head. Use a paintbrush handle to gently push a small dent into the side of the head to resemble a forehead. Make a tiny "U" impression, using the end of a drinking straw, to look like a closed eye.

11 Stick head on the pillow and place both on the cradle base. Add a small fondant oval for the body. Add a tiny peach ball for his ear and press a small hollow into it with the brush handle. Paint hair with food color.

12 Carefully stick the sides and the two ends of the cradle around the base using royal icing.

13 Make a tiny white fondant rectangle for the sheet and a larger blue one for the blanket.

14 Using the back of the knife, press a crisscross pattern into the blanket and lay it onto the edge of the white sheet, leaving about half the white still protruding. Fold the white back over the blue and lay the blanket over the baby.

15 Stick the canopy sections in place. Stick the rockers onto the base of the crib. (You could place a small ball of fondant underneath the cradle to add support while the rockers are drying).

16 Roll two white fondant balls and stick on the two ends of the crib. Stick a tiny bow on top of the canopy. Leave to dry for 24 hours.

a

b

c

Piped flowers ③

A spiral of pretty piped flowers wind their way around the cake. You could make the flowers up to a month in advance. You can cover the cake with fondant and use sponge instead of fruit cake if you prefer. Instructions are given below.

ingredients

(See "Covering the cake" for the amount of icing required to cover cake)

6" (15-cm) round fruit or sponge cake (see pages 10 and 14)

1 quantity royal icing (see page 90)

Pink, purple, green, yellow food color pastes

equipment

8" (20-cm) round cake board

Scissors

Wax paper or baking parchment

No. 57, 58 or 59 petal piping nozzles

Piping bags (see page 96)

Small bowls for mixing colors

Icing nail (or a cork stuck onto a long nail)

No. 2 piping nozzle

Leaf nozzle

Fine paintbrush

techniques

Covering a cake with marzipan, pages 85–86/fondant, page 61/royal icing, page 94

Piping blossom flowers, page 99

Piping a snail trail, page 98

Piping leaves, page 98

COVERING THE CAKE

Fruit cake with marzipan and royal icing: follow the instructions on pages 86 and 94. Use about 1 lb 4 oz (600 g) marzipan and two quantities of royal icing. When the cake has hardened, cover the cake board with royal icing as well (see page 95).

Fruitcake with marzipan and fondant: follow the instructions on pages 85 and 61. Use about 1 lb 4 oz (600 g) marzipan and 1 lb 2 oz (500 g) white fondant. Moisten the marzipan with water before covering it with the fondant. Cover the cake board using the bandage method shown on page 62.

Sponge cake with fondant: split and fill the cake with buttercream then spread buttercream around the outside. Roll out 1 lb 2 oz (500 g) white fondant and cover the cake. Cover the board using the bandage method shown on page 62.

1 Cut out at least 40 wax paper squares. Place a petal nozzle into a piping bag. Add 2 tablespoons of pink or purple icing. Fold the end of the bag over to close it.

2 Stick a paper square onto the top of the piping nail with a dab of icing. With the thick end of the piping nozzle in the center of the flower, squeeze the bag and turn the nail. Slightly lift the thin edge of the nozzle as you turn, to form a petal. Release the pressure and pull away.

3 Wipe the end of the nozzle. Tuck the nozzle just underneath the edge of the first petal and pipe a second. Repeat making five petals (Fig. a). It is tricky and you will need practice.

4 Make about 20 pink and 20 purple flowers and leave them to dry on the wax paper backings for at least 24 hours.

5 When the flowers are ready, place about two tablespoons of white royal icing into a piping bag fitted with the number 2 piping nozzle. Pipe a "snail trail" around the base of the cake. Squeeze a little icing out of the bag, release the pressure and pull slightly to the side, so that the icing tapers and falls onto the cake. Continue like this until you have piped around the whole base.

6 Using a little watered down food color, paint a spiral guideline around the cake. Start at the base of the cake and work around. Try to keep the width between the lines fairly equal (Fig. b).

7 Peel the backing paper off the flowers and stick the flowers onto the cake with dabs of royal icing.

8 Place about 1 tablespoon of yellow royal icing in a piping bag with a number 2 piping nozzle. Pipe a dot in the center of each flower.

9 Place a leaf nozzle in a piping bag and add 2 tablespoons of green royal icing. Pipe leaves between the flowers. Squeeze the icing out, release the pressure and pull to create a leaf shape.

a   b

tip

You could make the summer flowers on page 46 from royal icing and use these to decorate the cake with instead.

An easier, but still effective alternative to using piped flowers would be to use fondant plunge cutter blossoms (see page 65).

Snowflakes ③

These snowflakes are made using the royal icing "runout" technique used on the Baby's cradle on page 108. If you don't think you could cope with all the piping you could cut snowflake shapes out of rice paper. If you prefer, you can use sponge instead of fruit cake and cover with fondant instead of royal icing.

ingredients

(See "Covering the cake" for the amount of icing required to cover cake)

8" (20-cm) round fruit or sponge cake (see pages 10 and 14)

2 quantities white royal icing (for snowflakes; see page 90)

Blue food color paste

equipment

10" (25-cm) round cake board

Pencil

Tracing or wax paper

Baking parchment

Board or tray

Adhesive tape

Small cups/bowls

Palette knife

Piping bags (see page 96)

No. 1 and 2 piping nozzles

Scissors

techniques

Covering a cake with marzipan, pages 85–86/ fondant, page 61/royal icing, page 94

Runouts, page 100

Piping a snail trail, page 98

COVERING THE CAKE

Fruit cake with marzipan and royal icing: see pages 86 and 94. Use about 1 lb 10 oz (750 g) marzipan and two quantities royal icing. Stir a little blue food color into the royal icing before coating the cake and board.

Fruit cake with marzipan and fondant: follow the instructions on pages 85 and 61. Use about 1 lb 10 oz (750 g) marzipan and 1lb 10 oz (750 g) pale blue colored fondant. Moisten the marzipan with water before covering it with the fondant. Cover the exposed cake board using the leftover fondant and the bandage technique shown on page 62.

Sponge cake with fondant: split and fill the cake with buttercream then spread buttercream around the outside. Roll out and cover the cake with 1 lb 10 oz (750 g) of pale blue colored fondant. Cover the exposed cake board with the leftover fondant using the bandage technique shown on page 62.

tip

> The snowflakes can be made well in advance, so you can prepare them before the Christmas panic sets in.

1 Trace the snowflake templates on page 101 onto tracing paper. Place a piece of wax paper onto something flat such as a board or tray and hold it in place with a piece of tape at each corner. Slide the tracing paper underneath the wax paper (see Fig. a page 109).

2 Place about 1 tablespoon of white royal icing into a cup and beat it thoroughly with a knife to expel any air. Stir in a couple of drops of water to help it flow through the tiny piping nozzle more easily. The icing should still hold its shape when piped.

3 Place the icing into a piping bag fitted with a number 1 piping nozzle. Pipe over the outlines of the snowflakes. Pipe at least 16 outlines to allow for breakages (see Fig. a on page 109).

4 Place about 2 tablespoons of royal icing into a bowl. Add a few drops of water and mix in. Continue to add water, drop by drop, and mix it in until the icing has reached such a consistency that when you lift the knife out, the tail it leaves behind disappears on a count of three.

5 Tip or spoon the icing into a piping bag. Close the bag and snip a tiny triangle off the end. Gently squeeze the end and using a gentle wiggling motion, fill one of the shapes (see Fig. a page 109). Use the tip of a soft, damp paintbrush to coax it into any obstinate corners. Leave the shapes to dry for at least 24 hours.

6 Place about 1 tablespoon of royal icing into a piping bag fitted with a number 2 piping nozzle. Pipe a "snail trail" around the base of the cake. Squeeze a bit of icing out, release the pressure and pull slightly to the side so that the icing forms a tail. Repeat all the way around the cake (Fig. a).

7 When the snowflakes are dry, slide a palette knife beneath them to gently ease them off the paper (Fig. b).

8 Place the snowflakes into position and stick with dabs of royal icing.

9 Pipe royal icing dots between the snowflakes to finish off (Fig. c).

a   b   c

CHOCOLATE

As well as being delicious, chocolate is extremely versatile too. It can be used to cover a cake, molded into decorations and mixed with cream to make ganache. This chapter contains ideas for all sorts of occasions. There's even a simple recipe for truffles that uses up all those bits of leftover cake (see page 118).

Types of chocolate

There are four basic grades of chocolate to choose from and all are available in dark, milk or white forms. I would advise that you use either dessert or baking chocolate as they are easy to handle.

DESSERT OR EATING CHOCOLATE This is the product you'll find in the candy store. Dark chocolate has the strongest flavor and tends to be quite hard when you bite into it. Milk chocolate is softer to the bite and sweeter. White is sweeter still and actually doesn't taste of chocolate at all. All of these types can be used in cooking. A purist would argue that you should only use dark chocolate containing at least 70% cocoa solids for cooking, but it is your choice.

COUVERTURE OR COVERING CHOCOLATE Because it is made entirely with cocoa butter, couverture is the most expensive type of chocolate and is considered by most experts to be the best chocolate to use in cooking. However, it must be tempered (heated and cooled to an exact temperature) before use so it's not that easy for a beginner to use.

BAKING/COOKING CHOCOLATE This type of chocolate melts easily and is ideal for the beginner. The taste varies from brand to brand and, in fact, some supermarket brands are now so good it is very hard to tell them apart from dessert chocolate.

CHOCOLATE FLAVORED CAKE COVERING This is not actually chocolate at all, it is merely chocolate-flavored. The taste is weak and it tends to have a soft and greasy texture. It melts and sets very quickly, which can be useful if you are in a hurry. Because it is much cheaper than any other type of chocolate it may be worth using to experiment with, particularly if you have never worked with chocolate before.

Melting chocolate

When melting chocolate you must not get any water, steam or condensation in the chocolate. If you do, it will become thick, gritty and unusable.

1 Break the chocolate into small pieces and place in a heatproof bowl (Fig. a).

2 Place the bowl over a saucepan of water. The water should not touch the base of the bowl. Heat the water and simmer until the chocolate has melted (Fig. b).

Alternative method
Break the chocolate into pieces into a bowl that is microwave-safe. Heat on high for 90 seconds. Stir and repeat. Don't let it overcook otherwise it will burn.

RIGHT *You can make all sorts of decorations using chocolate, all of which are very easy to make. These include chocolate leaves, runouts, squiggles and shapes. See page 117 for instructions.*

Covering a cake with melted chocolate

A simple way to cover a cake is to pour chocolate over it. The cake can be plain or pre-iced with ganache.

1 Place the cake on a rack and pour the chocolate over the top (Fig. a). The cake must be at room temperature.

2 Lightly bang the rack up and down a few times to encourage the chocolate to fully cover the cake and to dislodge any air bubbles (Fig. b). Leave to set.

Chocolate ganache

Ganache is a spread made out of a mixture of cream and melted chocolate. Made using white or dark chocolate, it can be used to fill and cover gateau-type cakes, but would not normally be used with fondant designs.

ingredients
10 oz (300 g) dark or white chocolate, broken into pieces
2⅓ cups (600 ml) heavy cream

1 Place the broken chocolate into a large bowl.

2 Gently heat the cream in a saucepan and bring up to boiling point. Remove from the heat and pour over the chocolate.

3 Leave for 3 minutes then stir until the chocolate has melted.

4 Leave to cool completely then whisk to a light, whipped consistency. Cover and place in the fridge for at least half an hour or until required.

5 When ready to use, remove from the fridge. If it is still a little sloppy, beat until thick.

Piping with ganache
It is also possible to pipe with chocolate ganache. You could pipe a milk chocolate border onto a cake that has been covered in white chocolate, or vice versa (Fig. c). Add some chocolate leaves or a few chocolate-dipped fruits for a stylish yet simple cake for a special occasion.

Chocolate leaves

An effective decoration that is incredibly easy to make.

1 Select some well proportioned rose leaves. Wash and dry them on absorbent paper towels.

2 Melt some chocolate (see page 114). Hold a leaf by the stalk and press the underside (this side produces a better vein effect) into the melted chocolate. Leave to dry on wax paper.

3 When the leaves have set, carefully peel the real leaf off the chocolate one (see Fig. b on page 136).

Dipped fruits

You can use plain, milk or white chocolate and many different kinds of fruit, including strawberries, grapes, cherries and red currants.

1 Wash and dry the fruit on absorbent paper towels. Melt the chocolate (see page 114).

2 Dip the fruit into the chocolate so that it is half covered. Leave to set on wax paper (Fig. d).

Chocolate runouts

Another way to make simple shapes is to make runouts. The basic principle is exactly the same as that for making royal icing runouts (see page 100). You can vary the colors too—pipe an outline with dark chocolate and fill it with white, for example.

1 Place some melted chocolate into a piping bag. Fold the end of the bag to close it and snip a triangle off the end.

2 Pipe the outline of a simple shape, such as a heart, onto wax paper or baking parchment.

3 Place some more melted chocolate in another bag. Snip a bigger triangle off the end and fill in the chocolate outline (Fig. e).

Chocolate shapes

There are a couple of ways of making decorative chocolate shapes and both are very simple.

Solid shapes

Cut the shapes you want out of rice paper. Dip one side of the rice paper shape into melted chocolate. Leave to dry. As it is edible, you can either leave the paper on or peel it off. This technique is used and explained in full in the Chocolate shapes and Chocolate extravaganza cakes on pages 130 and 134.

Squiggles or shape outlines

Simply pipe the shape, using melted chocolate, onto a sheet of wax paper. Leave to set.

Chocolate modelling paste

There are all sorts of different ways of making chocolate modelling paste, but the easiest way to make it is to knead some cocoa powder into a piece of marzipan. There are no hard and fast rules about amounts; obviously the more you add, the darker the color will be. Use as normal marzipan (see page 88).

If the marzipan is hard to knead, microwave it for 10–15 seconds to soften it. Repeat if necessary but don't overdo it, otherwise the oils in the marzipan could get very hot and burn.

Quick chocolate rose

This is a very simple way to make a rose using chocolate modelling paste. Of course, it would work using uncolored marzipan and fondant too (Fig. a).

1 Take about ½ oz (15 g) of chocolate marzipan. Roll it into a thin sausage shape.

2 Flatten the sausage shape into a thin strip. Press along one long edge to make it thinner. Paint a line of water along the other long edge.

3 Carefully roll the marzipan up like a bandage, the thinnest edge should form the flower.

4 Tweak the edges slightly to improve the rose shape.

Chocolate truffles

This is a great way to use up those leftover pieces of cake. This recipe works equally well using sponge, chocolate or fruit cake and with any type of chocolate.

1 Break up the cake into crumbs and place in a bowl.

2 Melt some chocolate. You will need approximately 1 oz (30 g) of chocolate for every 1 oz (30 g) of cake crumb.

3 Stir the chocolate into the crumbs (Fig. b).

4 Roll the mixture into balls. Place in petit fours cases if you wish.

5 Decorate with melted chocolate and sweets.

Templates

All of the templates are shown at 100%.

Patterns for plaques.

Cocoa painting
(pages 126–127)
Make five.

Chocolate shapes (pages 130–131)
Make nine of each shape.

Quick chocolate cake ❶

This cake has been decorated using techniques that granny would have used. It's a traditional cake that's perfect for afternoon tea—it looks just perfect, yet is so simple.

ingredients

Two 7" (18-cm) chocolate cakes baked in
   sandwich pans or 1 cake baked in a
   normal cake pan, cut in half (see
   page 12)
1 quantity vanilla buttercream (see
   page 26)
1 tsp cocoa powder
Decoration for top of cake (store-bought
   lattice shapes/leaves/candies etc.)

equipment

Carving knife
Palette knife
8" (20-cm) round cake board or plate
Paper doily
Small sieve or tea strainer

techniques

Baking a cake, page 12
Making buttercream, page 26
Filling and covering a cake with
   buttercream, page 27

1 Split the cake horizontally in half. Sandwich the two cake layers together with a liberal spreading of buttercream. Place cake on board. Spread buttercream smoothly over the top of the cake.

2 Lay the paper doily on top of the cake. Place the cocoa powder in the sieve and gently tap it, moving it over the doily (Fig. a).

3 Carefully peel back the doily to reveal a pattern underneath (Fig. b).

4 Place a dab of buttercream and a few chocolate decorations in the center of the cake to finish off.

tips

Chocolate leaves are easy to make if you want to keep the whole design homemade. See page 117 to find out how to make them.

You can freeze the buttercreamed cake if you wish. Allow it to defrost thoroughly and make sure that all of the condensation has evaporated before decorating it with the cocoa.

Instead of cocoa you could decorate the cake with candies or chocolate buttons instead.

a

b

Marzipan chocolates ❶

This is a very easy cake to put together. The difficult part is stopping yourself from nibbling and sampling as you go!

ingredients

Powdered sugar, for rolling out

8 oz (250 g) golden marzipan

5 oz (150 g) milk chocolate

6" (15-cm) round sponge cake (see page 10

2 quantities chocolate buttercream (see page 26) or 1 quantity chocolate ganache (see page 116)

equipment

Rolling pin

Assorted cutters

Heatproof bowl

Small saucepan

Cooling rack

Carving knife

Palette knife

8" (20-cm) round cake board

techniques

Melting chocolate, page 114

Filling and covering a cake with buttercream or ganache, page 27 or 116

variation

Put a few marzipan chocolates into a box and create a lovely little present for someone.

1 Prepare the chocolates. Dust your work surface with powdered sugar and knead and roll out the marzipan to a thickness of about ¼" (5 mm). Using the cutters, cut out about 40 shapes (Fig. a).

2 Melt the milk chocolate in a heatproof bowl. Dip each shape into the chocolate and place on a cooling rack to harden (Fig. b).

3 When the chocolates are set, prepare the cake. Slice the cake into two or three layers and then sandwich back together with buttercream or ganache. Place the cake on a board.

4 Spread and swirl the icing over the outside of the cake. Press the marzipan shapes into the chocolate covering.

Easter cake ❶

Here's a cake that's simple to put together and will brighten up any Easter table.

chocolate

a

b

ingredients

50 g (1¾ oz) milk chocolate

50 g (1¾ oz) shredded wheat cereal

6" (15-cm) round sponge cake (see page 10)

1 quantity chocolate buttercream (see page 26)

Mini chocolate eggs

equipment

Heatproof bowl

Small saucepan

Small bowl to use as mold for nest

Carving knife

Palette knife

8" (20-cm) round cake board

About 6 chick cake decorations

techniques

Melting chocolate, page 114

Filling and covering a cake with buttercream, page 27

1 To make the nest, melt the chocolate and break up the cereal. Mix the two together and spoon the mixture into a small bowl (Fig. a). Leave to set.

2 To prepare the cake, level the top and turn the cake upside down. Split it into two or three layers and reassemble, filling the layers with buttercream.

3 Place the cake onto the cake board and cover the top, sides and exposed cake board with buttercream.

4 Press a line of chocolate eggs around the top and bottom of the cake (Fig. b).

5 When the nest has set, place it on top of the cake and fill with little chicks. You could add a few extra eggs as well if you wish.

tip

Instead of using store-bought chocolate eggs, you could make your own eggs out of fondant or use sugared almonds.

variation

This cake was decorated with an Easter teddy whose body is a chocolate egg.

Roll 1 oz (30 g) golden marzipan into a sausage for his legs. Place the egg in the center and bend the marzipan round it to hold the egg steady. Tweak the ends into feet.

Make a ½ oz (15 g) marzipan ball for his head and stick on top of the egg. Add a marzipan oval for his muzzle and two tiny balls for his ears. Press the end of a paintbrush into each ear and into the lower part of his muzzle to make a mouth. Add three black food color dots for his eyes and nose.

Make two ⅛ oz (5 g) sausage shapes for his arms and stick onto the body.

Warning! To avoid arguments it might be wise to make enough spare teddies so that everyone can have one!

Cocoa painting ❷

Cocoa painting is a traditional technique that's often overlooked nowadays. Of course, you don't have to paint a pattern on your cake, you could paint an actual picture, perhaps of a much-loved pet or place. The cocoa gives the image a sepia look, like that of an old photograph.

ingredients

10 oz (300 g) white fondant
Powdered sugar, for rolling out
1 tsp shortening
1 tsp cocoa powder
6" (15-cm) square sponge cake (see page 10)
2 quantities chocolate buttercream (see page 26)

equipment

Rolling pin
Cutter or template (see page 119) for plaques
Saucer
Small saucepan
Fine paintbrush
Scalpel
Carving knife
Palette knife
8" (20-cm) square cake board
Star piping nozzle (optional; see tip opposite)
Piping bag (see page 96)

techniques

Making a plaque, page 66
Filling and covering a cake with buttercream, page 27
Piping with buttercream, page 98

1 To make the plaques, roll out the fondant and cut out a thin oval, either with a cutter or using the template on page 119. Cut out four more, rekneading and rerolling the fondant as necessary. If you have time, leave them to harden for 12 hours, turning over after 5-6 hours.

2 To paint the plaques, melt a little shortening on a saucer over a pan of hot water. Remove the pan from the heat but leave the saucer in place while you work to keep the shortening.

3 Mix a little cocoa powder and melted shortening together with the paintbrush (Fig. a).

4 Lightly paint the outline of the picture onto a plaque and fill it in (Fig. b). If you do not want to paint the pattern freehand, trace the patterns on page 119 and scribe them onto the plaque (see page 99). Remember that you can always add more but you can't take it off, so build the picture up gradually.

5 If you want to create highlights or thin, line effects, you can scratch bits off with the tip of a clean, sharp scalpel (Fig. c).

6 Level the top of the cake and turn it upside down. Slice into two or three layers and reassemble it, filling the layers with buttercream.

7 Place the cake onto the cake board and spread buttercream over the top and sides. Spread buttercream over the exposed areas of the cake board as well.

8 Place the plaques into position. Press them gently into the buttercream to hold them in place.

9 Place a star piping nozzle into a piping bag and spoon 2–3 tablespoons of buttercream into the bag. Pipe around the outsides of the plaques and the edges and base of the cake. Vary the shades of brown, if you wish, by adding more cocoa to the buttercream.

tips

If you don't want to pipe buttercream onto the cake, stick chocolate buttons or other chocolate candies around it instead.

Use white candles in white birthday cake candleholders and stand them in the chocolate buttercream on top of the cake. Don't try to poke them through the fondant plaque.

a

b

c

Chocolate feathers ❷

You can make the chocolate feathers a few days in advance if you wish. Just store them somewhere dry where people won't be tempted to pinch them.

ingredients

4 oz (100 g) milk chocolate

4 oz (100 g) plain chocolate

4 oz (100 g) white chocolate

8" (20-cm) round sponge cake (see page 10)

2 quantities white chocolate buttercream (see page 26) or 1 quantity white chocolate ganache (see page 116)

equipment

Wax paper or baking parchment

Tray

Heatproof bowls for melting chocolate

Small saucepan

About 6 piping bags (see page 96)

Cup

Scissors

Sharp pointed knife

Carving knife

Palette knife

10" (25-cm) round cake board

techniques

Melting chocolate, page 114

Making a piping bag, page 97

Filling and covering a cake with buttercream, page 27

1 Make the feathers first so that they have time to harden. Place a large sheet of wax paper on a tray. Melt the milk chocolate in a bowl either in a microwave or over a pan of simmering water.

2 Place a piping bag into a cup and tip in some of the chocolate. Carefully fold over the ends of the bag to close it and snip a tiny triangle off the end.

3 Pipe a thick line (it can be either straight or wavy) of chocolate onto the wax paper (Fig. a). It's not essential to use a bag, you can drizzle a line with a spoon if you prefer, but a bag makes things much easier and is less sticky.

4 Using the tip of a sharp knife, poke and drag the chocolate from the center of the line outward to make a point. Continue down both sides of the line fanning the chocolate outward (Fig. b). Make about 20 to allow for breakages and chocolate thieves!

5 Repeat procedure with the dark and white chocolate and leave to harden in a cool, dry place.

6 When the feathers are ready, prepare the cake. Level the top and turn it upside down. Slice it into two or three horizontal layers and reassemble it, sandwiching the layers together with buttercream.

7 Put cake onto cake board. Spread buttercream around the sides and top of the cake.

8 Gently slide a palette knife under a feather and ease it off the backing paper. Place the feather in position on the cake. Make a ring around the base and top of the cake and place a few in the center.

tips

Make the piped lines of chocolate quite thick. If the feathers are too thin, they'll just snap and be impossible to use. You can also mix colors by piping a line of milk and white chocolate together.

Candles should be placed in holders inside the top ring of feathers but away from the central ones. Use white candles and holders.

chocolate

Chocolate shapes ②

Dipping rice paper into melted chocolate is an easy way to make effective chocolate shapes. Because the rice paper is edible, you can either leave it on the back or peel it off when they've hardened.

ingredients

Rice paper

3½ oz (100 g) milk chocolate

3½ oz (100 g) dark chocolate

6" (15-cm) round sponge cake (see page 10)

2 quantities white chocolate buttercream (see page 26) or 1 quantity white chocolate ganache (see page 116)

equipment

Pencil

Rice paper

Scissors

Wax paper or baking parchment

Tray

Heatproof bowl

Small saucepan

2 piping bags (see page 96)

8" (20-cm) round cake board

techniques

Melting chocolate, page 114

Filling and covering a cake with buttercream, page 27

1 Using rice paper, trace and cut out about nine each of the heart, square, circle, moon and star templates (see page 119). Cut just inside the pencil marks.

2 Place some baking parchment or wax paper on to a tray.

3 Melt the milk chocolate. Dip a rice paper shape into the chocolate (Fig. a). Coat one side, then place onto the tray.

4 Make four or five shapes. Holding both edges of the tray, bang it on your work surface a couple of times to dislodge any air bubbles.

5 Repeat this procedure until half of the rice paper shapes have been used.

6 Tip any leftover melted chocolate into a piping bag. Fold the end to close it and snip a tiny triangle off the end. Pipe a squiggle directly onto the covered tray (Fig. b).

7 Repeat the above procedure with the dark chocolate.

8 When the chocolate shapes have set, prepare the cake. Slice it into three layers and reassemble, filling the layers with buttercream or ganache.

9 Put the cake onto the cake board. Spread a thick coating of buttercream or ganache around the outside of the cake.

10 Peel the rice paper off the shapes (or leave it on, it's up to you) and press them into the icing.

tips

If you're feeling really ambitious you could pipe the recipient's name in chocolate, either in single letters or in joined writing.

Only use a few candles and have them lit for as little time as possible as the heat might melt the chocolate.

a

b

Monster cup cake ❷

This cake is baked in a pudding bowl to give it its authentic shape. The enormous paper cake case is actually a paper cake pan liner which you can buy from kitchen or cake decoration equipment shops.

ingredients

1 chocolate pudding bowl cake (see page 10 and step 1 right)
Powdered sugar for rolling out
5 oz (150 g) white fondant
½ oz (15 g) red fondant
2¾ oz (75 g) grey fondant
Water for sticking
Black food color or black food color pen

equipment

6" (15-cm) round cake pan liner
Rolling pin
Sharp knife
Paintbrush
About an 7" (18-cm) round plate or cake board
6" (15-cm) round paper cake pan liner

techniques

Baking a pudding bowl cake, page 10
Working with fondant, page 60

1 Mix up a three-egg sponge mixture (see page 10). Add 1 tablespoon of cocoa. Place the liner in the bowl, turn the mixture into it and bake.

2 When the cake is cool, roll out the white fondant. Holding a sharp knife virtually upright, cut out a wiggly, vaguely circular shape for the white topping (Fig. a). Keep the excess.

3 Place the topping onto the cake. Roll about ⅓ oz (10 g) red fondant into a ball for the cherry, and stick onto the top of the cake with a dab of water.

4 To make the mouse, roll about 1½ oz (50 g) grey fondant into a conical shape for the mouse's body. Bend the pointed end over to form the head (Fig. b). Using the end of a paintbrush, poke an oval hole for his outraged mouth.

5 Make two ⅛ oz (5 g) oval shapes for the feet and stick either side of his body. Make a couple of tiny lines in the end of each foot with the tip of the knife.

6 Make two tiny white balls for the eyes and stick onto the head with little dabs of water. Add tiny black dots for the pupils using black food color and a fine brush or a black food color pen.

7 Knead a tiny bit of red fondant into a little bit of white to make a pink color. Make a tiny ball for the nose and a wiggly string for the tail. Stick both in position and press a few lines down the length of the tail.

8 Make two tiny grey strings for arms. Bend into "S" shapes and stick on the side of the body. Make two tiny grey ball shapes for the ears and stick on the side of the head. Poke the end of a paintbrush into each ear to both add definition and to push it securely onto the head.

9 Place the cake and the mouse in position on the plate or cake board. Use a dab of water to hold the mouse in place if necessary.

tip

To make a chocolate chip cake, stir a handful of chocolate chips into the cake mixture before baking.

Chocolate extravaganza ❷

Deceptively easy and devilishly tasty. There really is no better cake to make for the favorite chocoholic in your life! If you're prepared for a little bit more work, you could fill the top of the cake with homemade truffles (see page 118). Both versions of this cake would be ideal for Mother's Day.

a

b

ingredients

1 pack edible rice paper

5 oz (150 g) white chocolate

6" (15-cm) square sponge cake (see
   page 10)

1 quantity white chocolate buttercream
   (see page 26) or ganache (see
   page 116)

Assorted chocolates

equipment

Scissors

Wax paper or baking parchment

Tray

Heatproof bowl

Small saucepan

Carving knife

Palette knife

8" (20-cm) square cake board

1 yd (1 m) ribbon

techniques

Melting chocolate, page 114

Making chocolate shapes, page 117

Filling and covering a cake with
   buttercream, page 27

1 Cut rice paper into 24 rectangles about 1½" × 3" (4 × 8 cm). They must stand higher than the edge of the cake. Place some baking parchment onto a tray.

2 Melt the chocolate. Dip the smooth side of a rectangle shape into the chocolate (see Fig. a page 131). Place onto the tray.

3 Coat four or five rectangles then, holding both edges of the tray, bang it on your work surface a couple of times to dislodge any air bubbles. Repeat this procedure until all the rectangles have been covered. Leave to set.

4 To prepare the cake, level the top and turn it upside down. Slice into two or three layers and reassemble, filling the layers with buttercream or ganache.

5 Spread icing over the sides and top of the cake.

6 Peel the rice paper backing off the strips (Fig. a). It is edible, so you can leave it on if you find it too tricky to peel off.

7 Press the white chocolate strips around the sides of the cake, overlapping them as you go (Fig. b). Use six per side.

8 Fill the top with chocolates and gently tie a bow around the outside of the cake.

variation

Fill the top of the cake with rose blooms for an elegant, luxurious treat. Wash the flowers and leaves well with cold water and dry thoroughly on paper towel before using.

a

b

White chocolate ring ❷

Chocolate leaves are extremely simple to make and give the traditional, humble chocolate cake a lavish new look! You could use a mixture of dark, milk and white chocolate leaves if you wish.

ingredients

3½ oz (100 g) white chocolate

7" (18-cm) round sponge cake (see page 10)

1 quantity chocolate buttercream (see page 26) or ganache (see page 116)

equipment

About 25 rose leaves

Paper towels

Wax paper or baking parchment

Tray

Heatproof bowl

Carving knife

9" (23-cm) round plate or cake board

Palette knife

techniques

Melting chocolate, page 114

Filling and covering a cake with buttercream, page 27

1 Wash the rose leaves and dry them on absorbent paper towels. Place some wax paper or baking parchment on a tray. Melt the chocolate.

2 Holding a rose leaf by its stem, dip the underside of the leaf into the chocolate (Fig. a). Lay on the wax paper to dry.

3 To prepare the cake, slice it horizontally and fill with chocolate buttercream or ganache.

4 Place the cake onto a plate or cake board and spread a thick covering of buttercream or ganache over the top and sides.

5 When set, peel the rose leaves away from the chocolate (Fig b).

6 Gently press the leaves in a ring formation around the cake.

tip

If you want to add a bit of color, lay a few rosebuds around the edge of the plate.

variation

Construct this cake in exactly the same way, except place leaves over the top as well. Sprinkle the whole cake with a little sifted cocoa powder. You could make milk and plain chocolate leaves as well, if you wish.

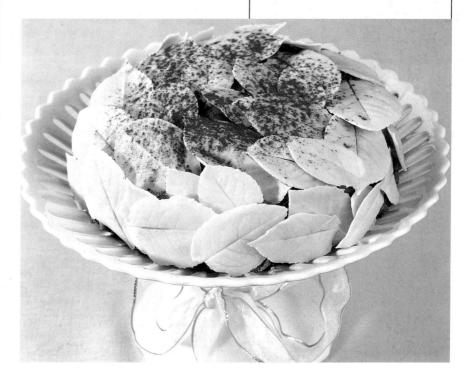

Choc 'n' nut ❷

Beware of this cake! It may be small, but it is incredibly rich and gorgeous. The use of store-bought hazelnut spread as a cake covering saves time. However, if you don't like nuts, you can use chocolate buttercream or ganache, smothered with vermicelli instead.

ingredients

6" (15-cm) round sponge cake (see page 10)
2 large jars hazelnut chocolate spread
¾ cup (100 g) chopped nuts
3 oz (90 g) golden marzipan
Cocoa powder
Black food color or black food color pen
1 nut (pecan, hazelnut etc.)

equipment

Carving knife
Palette knife
8" (20-cm) round cake board
Small, sharp knife
Fine paintbrush

techniques

Filling and covering a cake with buttercream, page 27
Modelling with marzipan, page 88

1 Level the top of the cake and slice the cake horizontally into two or three layers. Reassemble the cake, sandwiching it together with hazelnut spread. Place the cake onto the cake board.

2 Coat the top and sides of the cake liberally with hazelnut spread. Cover the exposed cake board too.

3 Carefully press handfuls of chopped nuts into the sides of the cake (Fig. a). You will get messy!

4 Put about ½ oz (15 g) of the marzipan aside for making the tail. Knead about 1 teaspoon of cocoa powder into the rest to turn it a dark brown color.

5 Make a 1 oz (30 g) conical shape for the squirrel's body. Bend the pointed end forwards slightly to make the head. Press a line into the head with a knife to make a mouth (Fig. b).

6 Make a ⅓ oz (10 g) chunky sausage shape for a leg. Squash one end to make the thigh and stick against the squirrel's body with a dab of water. Repeat on the other side with the second leg.

7 Make two tiny sausage shapes for arms. Stick onto the squirrel's body. Position a nut in front of his tummy and place his arms onto the nut so that it looks as though the squirrel's holding it.

8 Make two triangles for the ears and stick onto the head. Add two black food color dots for eyes.

9 Roll the leftover golden marzipan into a flat oval. Bend into an "S" shape and stick onto the back. Press a few lines into the tail with the back of a knife.

10 Place the squirrel onto the center of the cake and sprinkle a few nuts around it.

tip

Before covering the sides of the cake with the nuts, fold a sheet of wax paper in half. Open the paper up and stand the cake on top. When finished, remove the cake, lift the paper up, fold it in half and pour the excess nuts back into the packet.

a

b

INDEX

SUPPLIERS

American Cake Supply
522 N. Halleck
Demotte, IN 46310
(877) 779-CAKE
www.americancakesupply.com

Beryl's Cake Decorating &
 Pastry Supplies
P. O. Box 1584
North Springfield, VA 22151
(800) 488-2749
www.beryls.com

The Cake Box Bakery
342 N. Expressway
Griffin, GA 30223
(770) 412-1100
www.cakeboxbakery.com

Cake, Candy, & Wedding
 Supply Co.
204 3rd St. N.
Waite Park, MN 56387
(800) 850-9171
www.ccwsupply.com

Cakes by Jan
214 Hammond St.
Bangor, ME 04401
(207) 947-5155
www.cakesbyjan.com

Cakes Plus
3601 W. Kennedy Blvd., Ste. C
Tampa, FL 33609
(813) 876-1411
www.cakesplustampa.com

Candyland Crafts
201 W. Main St.
Somerville, NJ 08876
(908) 685-0410
www.candylandcrafts.com

Celebrate Cakes
4310 Saturn Rd.
Garland, TX 75041
(972) 271-4396
www.celebratecakes.com

The Confectionery House
975 Hoosick Rd.
Troy, NY 12180
(518) 279-3179
www.confectioneryhouse.com

Cooking.com
2850 Ocean Park Blvd., Ste. 310
Santa Monica, CA 90405
(800) 663-8810
www.cooking.com

Country Kitchen SweetArt
4621 Speedway Dr.
Fort Wayne, IN 46825
(800) 497-3927 (orders only)
www.countrykitchensa.com

The Decorette Shop
5338 S.E. Foster Rd.
Portland, OR 97206
(800) 728-CAKE
www.thedecoretteshop.com

Evelyn's Cake Decorating Supplies
1391 St. James St.
Winnipeg, Manitoba R3H 0Z1
Canada
(204) 774-8325
www.mts.net/~evelyns1

Gloria's Cake & Candy Supplies
3755 Sawtelle Blvd.
Los Angeles, CA 90066
(310) 391-4557
www.gloriascakecandysuplys.com

GM Cake & Candy Supplies
824 Cincinnati Ave.
Xenia, OH 45385
(937) 372-3205 or (937) 372-5272
www.cybercakes.com

Harvey's Hobby Hut
408 W. Water St.
Decorah, IA 52101
(877) 382-3435
www.harveyshobbyhut.com

Kitchen Krafts
P. O. Box 442-ORD
Waukon, IA 52172
(800) 776-0575
www.kitchenkrafts.com

Make-A-Cake
6218 Evergreen
Houston, TX 77081
(713) 777-1871
www.makeacakehouston.com

Marie's Party Palace
602 N. Maclay Ave.
San Fernando, CA 91340
(818) 365-3606

McCall's School of Cake Decoration
3810 Bloor St. W.
Etobicoke, Ontario, M9B 6C2
Canada
(416) 231-8040
www.mccalls-cakes.com

Midwest Craft & Cake Supply Inc.
2610 E. University Ave.
Des Moines, IA 50317
(515) 266-2424
www.claytonsdm.com

Oasis Supply Co.
P.O. Box 578
1448 Ford Rd., Bldg C
Bensalem, PA 19020
(800) 441-3141
www.oasisupply.com

Party Art, Inc.
101 Meadow Dr., Ste. E
Cumming, GA 30040
(770) 887-4944
www.partyinc.com

Pattycakes, Inc.
34-55 Junction Blvd.
Jackson Heights, NY 11372
(718) 651-5770
www.pattycakes.com

Spun Sugar
1611 University Ave.
Berkeley, CA 94703
(510) 843-9192
www.spunsugar.com

Sugarcraft, Inc.
2715 Dixie Hwy.
Hamilton, OH 45015
www.sugarcraft.com

Sweet Celebrations Inc.
7009 Washington Ave., S.
Edina, MN 55439
(800) 328-6722
www.sweetc.com

Sweet Designs by Victoria
1224 S. Federal Hwy.
Lake Worth, FL 33460
(561) 582-7999
www.gardian.com/weddingcakes

Tapp's Cake Emporium
6170 Broadview Rd.
Parma, OH 44134
(216) 398-9499
www.sweetsupplies.com

The Ultimate Baker
2829 East 29th
Spokane, WA 99223
(866) 285-COOK
www.cooksdream.com

Verna's Cake Decorating Supplies
2346 Massachusetts Ave.
Cambridge, MA 02140
(617) 864-7745
www.vernas.com

Wilton Industries
2240 W. 75th St.
Woodridge, IL 60517
(800) 794-5866
www.wilton.com

Winbeckler Enterprises
16849 S.E. 240th St.
Kent, WA 98042
www.winbeckler.com

Wine and Cake Hobbies, Inc.
6527 Tidewater Dr.
Norfolk, VI 23509
(757) 857-0245
www.wineandcake.com